Divine Felines

Spiritual Lessons From Our Feline Friends

Lara Germony

Doodlebug Publications

ISBN: 979-8-218-13344-3

Cover design by Heather Paul | artofheatherpaul.com
Interior layout and editing by Ink Drinker Editing and Literary Services | inkdrinkerliterary.com

First printing edition 2023

Doodlebug Publications
doodlebug.manor@yahoo.com

Contents

Introduction

My fascination with felines began at a young age. I admire their grace and composure, the fluid way they move, and the quiet determination they exhibit. Through my experiences with my own cats, I have learned to cherish them as amazing companions, friends, and listeners while enjoying their unique wit and intelligence. The sound of a cat purring soothes away the stress of the day and provides comfort. Their ability to engage you with a thoughtful gaze or intuitively respond to your energy when no words are spoken is priceless. For all the loyalty and unconditional love they offer, they make such purrfect companions. Perhaps they offer us more than we do them.

It's for this reason that the horrific state of so many animals in the world breaks my heart daily. From the loss of natural habitat threatening their existence, to the mistreatment of livestock and wild animals, to the negligent eye turned to those suffering in the streets, this sacred discontent kept me awake many nights. Then one day, I knew what I could do to make a difference.

God called my heart to work for the lives of cats. God called me to start a shelter, and then, over two decades later, God called me to write this book. From feral or wild cats eliminated in communities, to the number of kittens born who die within the first few weeks, to those euthanized in county and local shelters due to overpopulation. (If you think it's an exaggeration, place a bowl of cat food and water outside your home and watch the number of stray or abandoned cats who will find you.)

You can join in our mission to save the lives of cats; 50% of all profits from this book will go to support my 501 (c) (3) nonprofit rescue, Doodlebug Manor.

It's for this reason that I wrote this empowering book for spiritual people who love cats. If you're ready to take your faith life to the next level with lessons from cats, while expanding your knowledge from a veteran cat rescuer of 25+ years, and without leaving your favorite chair at home, then this read is for you.

This book is also for you if you:

- Believe cats have more to teach us than we do them
- Want to block out the noise of others and sink into your favorite chair with a heart-warming book
- Are ready to enhance your spiritual practices in a new, unique way

However, this book is not for you if:

- You don't believe animals have souls
- The survival of stray cats in the world doesn't concern you
- You believe that spiritual disciplines are restricted

only to your bible and traditional devotionals

In the following pages, you'll find heartwarming tales of cats taken from my years of service in rescue, and the different lessons they taught me about God and other mysteries of faith. Each story also oozes practical tips and tools for serving the cats of your home and neighborhood; for what good is a heart that is touched but not equipped to act?!

As you read, please know that I am with you not only in spirit, but also online. Connect with me with questions and 'aha moments' on Facebook @Lara Germony and/or https://doodlebugmanor.webs.com/

Cats Come First

"As anyone who has ever been around a cat for any length of time knows, cats have enormous patience with the limitations of humankind." — Cleveland Amory

“I’m sorry, but this isn’t going to work out.” Anyone who just witnessed the family drama unfolding on the front steps of the rescue along with us would call that a gross understatement, but it had to be said.

A family of potential adopters, parents and two pre-teen children, arrived for their appointment to meet the cats and kittens at Doodlebug Manor that afternoon. We reviewed and verified their application, conducted the phone interview, and were on the third step, where they met our adoptable cats to see if there was a match.

This is where things went horribly wrong.

During the meet and greet, we observe a host of things: How do they approach the cats? What is their interest level? Do they have an interest in a particular cat, and how does the cat react to them?

Beyond this, we are using the time to reconfirm what they've stated, focusing on those questions that are disqualifying conditions. (Questions such as: "Do you plan to declaw?" "Where will the cat spend their days/nights?" "Does anyone in the household have allergies?") When things were genuine and we found a good match for adoption, we moved to the contract and progressed to adoption.

During this meeting, we talked for a few minutes about the different cats and what they were looking for in their new pet. Then the father sniffled, his eyes watering and turning a bright shade of pink.

"Are you alright?" I inquired.

"Fine, fine," he answered, and began hacking.

"Really," I stated, "why don't you take a minute to step outside and get some air?"

Still reassuring me he was fine, he stepped out. I hurried over to close the door behind him to prevent the cats from wandering out. I turned to find his wife began having similar symptoms. (*Mental eye roll)*

"Really," I stated, "please step outside."

"Yes, I'd better check on him," she said.

Moving in a stumbling motion toward the door, she stepped out. I closed the door behind her as well, but not before overhearing talk of an inhaler and perhaps a trip to the ER. (Really?*)*

As the parents were carrying on mid-porch, the oldest child began to mimic the same behavior, with his little brother falling in line. (O*kay, enough).* I told the kids to step outside to the front porch, so they could join the off-Broadway production being performed there, and announced that the visit was over.

"Clearly you all have allergies," I stated, as I joined them outside. "This is why we ask you on the application and confirm with you again if anyone in your home has allergies." My voice portrayed a higher level of patience than I was feeling.

Having regained some control, the father looked over and stated somewhat sheepishly. "Yeah, I was allergic as a kid, but I thought I'd outgrown it."

I had no comment at first, but simply stated, "Well, I'm sorry it isn't going to work out. I hope you're all feeling better soon."

With that, I escorted them away from the rescue to their car. The sooner they left the cats, the better. I couldn't decide whether to give in to the aggravation of the time wasted and the hope for an adoption lost, or the laughter tugging at the sides of my mouth.

Sharing the story with my husband, Gregg, that evening, the peals of laughter won out. We laughed until it hurt, pondering the question, "*what was that!?*"

We'll never be sure what that family had hoped to accomplish. Maybe they believed they'd completed the application, and that was it, we guaranteed them a cat? Or maybe they thought with the number of cats needing homes, we'd be grateful for their interest and just give them a cat? Maybe it was just a test to see if they could adopt a cat and survive?

It can be hard as Christians in the world of rescue, telling people no and feeling like it causes a conflict or an uncomfortable conversation. Denying people something they want or feel entitled to can result in adversarial behavior or even retaliation. There are as many reasons to say no as there are people and situations. Those stories alone would fill a volume.

While it isn't always easy, we will always do what is in the best interests of the welfare and happiness of the cats. Their wellbeing comes first. (Think of it similar to the disclaimer on the back of the hair dryer box, warning people not to use it in the shower: someone, somewhere, made that disclaimer necessary!)

Yes Virginia, rescuers say no. The cats come first.

The stories in this book will be filled with thought-pattern disrupting, paradigm-shifting moments that are prompted by real life experiences in the world of cat rescue.

> Rescue the weak and the needy; deliver them from the hand of the wicked. Psalm 82:4

> Let each of you look not only to his own inter-

ests, but also to the interests of others. Philippians 2:4

Josie

My Mentor

"I have studied many philosophers and many cats. The wisdom of cats is infinitely superior." —Hippolyte Taine

Returning from a quick run to the grocery store, arms loaded down with bags and climbing the front steps toward the door, a loud yowling sound stopped me in my tracks.

A very determined sound was coming at me from under the steps. Looking down, my eyes met those of a slender, gray-striped tabby cat looking back at me intently. Her head was poking out between the bottom two steps, and her gaze was direct, ensuring she had my attention. My eyes on her, she issued another of the loud MEOWs and held my gaze. (I speak cat fluently these days, but at that time I interpreted this as "Did you hear what I said?")

Her demeanor indicated that this was less of a 'welcome to the neighborhood' visit and more of a mission of intent on her part. There was something she wanted, and she had chosen me to assist her. In hindsight, I realize that she had been chosen to guide and educate me, a guiding soul as our story unfolded, but more on that to come. (Are they not all ministering spirits sent out to serve for the sake of those who are to inherit salvation? Hebrews 1:14)

Being newly married and recently relocated, my primary focus was learning my way around the area. My thoughts were full of errands to run and other things on my to do list, making this encounter a complete surprise.

Offering a return greeting, I inquired of this friendly kitty what had brought her to my door today? Asking her to wait a moment, I deposited the grocery bags on my kitchen counter, then returned with a large bowl of freshwater and a bowl of cat food to offer my new friend. (Cat food courtesy of our indoor cats.)

Placing the bowls at a polite distance between us, as she was poised slightly under the first step, I encouraged her to eat. Stepping back slowly to give her a more comfortable space, I blinked at her slowly to signal trust, then waited and watched.

With one eye trained on me warily at first, she ate. Here was a medium-sized gray tabby, with beautiful, huge, green eyes framed by that small, slightly angular face and the telltale "M" marking on her forehead of the tabby clan. She was a good weight, maybe a little thin, but not starved. She had dainty paws and long whiskers for her size.

Cats typically have 24 whiskers on their muzzle, distributed with twelve on each side. The length of their whiskers is proportionate to the width of their average body weight. The whiskers transmit information about the size, shape, and speed of nearby objects, which helps them navigate their environment, especially at night. When approaching a narrow opening, if the whiskers fit through, so will their body! Cats have a limited sense of sight, especially up close, so the whiskers constantly signal the brain and help cats to "see" objects.

She wore no identifying collar or tag, there was no visible pet house within sight making it difficult to determine if she was someone's pet or free roaming. It was true enough that people in middle Tennessee tended to let their cats run outside. We'd already seen many of them in the neighborhood.

Noting no visible signs of distress or injury ruled out any type of medical emergency. Her demeanor didn't indicate any pain or discomfort. Her eyes were clear and expressive, her coat looked clean and unruffled. She ate heartily, her body posture relaxed, and she seemed satisfied with the offering. I felt good knowing I had interpreted her request correctly; food and water were the answer.

I wondered where she came from and if she was living under our stairs, or somewhere nearby. *Did she belong to a neighbor who let her out in the mornings? Had she escaped through a busy front door? Maybe she did this when she saw someone outside and accessible?* I stayed and observed her a little longer to see what I might learn about my new visitor.

Posing my questions to her, she would respond with an occasional glance or ear twitch. I took this as her acknowledging me but not offering any real answers.

As a Christ follower, I am no stranger to the blessings of a guiding soul God sends to guide us, just as we are called to help those who come to us in need. Knowing He often speaks to us through our hearts, it seems natural that He sends animals as these messengers into my life, as He might send people to others. Whether they gain influence over time, or arrive unexpectedly, they are the souls that support, love, and teach us along the way, and if we're very blessed, it can be reciprocal. This was the case with Josie and me.

Since we were newfound friends, she would need a proper name to be addressed by. A list of potential names began streaming through my mind as I searched for the right one to capture the spirit of this confident, outgoing girl. (Her lack of response as I shared them out loud solidified this.)

"Well, you're no help," I said to her ironically. "Give me a hint."

Cocking my head to the side, considering her demeanor and energy, it came to me instantly.

"Josie!" I exclaimed. "You are the perfect Josie, eh?"

Her direct, fleeting eye contact was my reward, and her consent. My new friend would be called Josie.

I didn't foresee it just then, but my relationship with Josie would blossom into a friendship that would endure, and guide us through many adventures, a little heartache, and numerous joys together.

It turned out that Josie didn't belong to anyone in the neighborhood; instead, the neighborhood was hers. Many of the neighbors recognized her and were accustomed to seeing her around, but no one was quite sure how she had come to be there or much of her history at all.

Josie was a soul at peace in her existence. It was common to observe her casually strolling through a front yard, then gracefully folding herself under a large shade tree to seek refuge from the hot summer sun. She strolled along the banks of the small tree-lined ravine along the back of the community, stopping to stretch, then resumed her long, slow strides. She was a fierce hunter when the situation called for it. Any unsuspecting creature moving nearby in the brush, or ducking out from under a leaf, would become all too aware of her prowess and lightning-fast reflexes.

Her daily ritual included making the rounds from one home to another where she knew some food scraps or treats awaited her. There might be a hunting expedition through the open grass fields with a friend, or just a head pat and some kind words to send her on her way. Regardless of where the day would take her, eventually she made her way back around to our house. Her food and water dishes were now a permanent fixture in the grassy nook beside our backdoor stairs.

Ours was a comfortable friendship. Some days Josie would greet me in the early morning, and we would share a few moments over coffee. (Well, I had coffee; she preferred water!) We might chat a little, or just sit together and enjoy the quiet before the neighborhood came alive with its usual morning activity. Some evenings, I would see her return to grab a bite and rest in the yard. Our shared times together were always easy and dependent on Josie's schedule. As the girl about town, she had places to go and people to see. Even on the days we didn't meet up, I knew she was around.

Big changes arrived one day in the middle of spring.

As Josie was rounding the corner on her way over to our meeting spot, I noticed an off-kilter swagger in her gait. She was steady on her feet but appeared to almost 'shift' from side to side while walking. It was as if Josie had gained weight or was carrying something heavy that drew her toward the ground. As she got closer, the telltale swell of her belly gave it away. She was pregnant!

This was new territory. I had no prior experience with an expecting cat, let alone one who was highly independent and preferred to live outside. (The inexperience was the reason it took an obvious display for me to understand what she was expecting.) Josie obviously knew her way around and how to take care of herself, but it was a whole different matter when there would soon be babies totally dependent on her for their welfare in the outdoors.

Dangers facing cats trying to survive outside are many, not to mention how very dependent tiny kittens are on their momma. The kittens and Josie would need us to look out for them, and to bring the kittens inside to survive. We were all too aware of the dangers of life outdoors for kittens, ranging from predators to terrible illnesses and more. Cats living outside rely heavily on their wits to survive. Many adults struggle, and some can't adapt, ending in their demise. Josie would be at a much higher risk of falling victim to these dangers with young ones to look after and protect, and the kittens themselves would be 100% at risk.

The challenge laid before me, but the solution was not as clear. Despite our bond, I had never attempted to coerce her into doing anything she didn't choose to do. This included removing her kittens when they were old enough to come inside and be socialized. (You only took as much care of Josie as she allowed, and now there would be babies involved.) Ultimately, the goal was to prepare Josie's kittens to have a more secure lifestyle than Josie was accustomed to.

Now, with the babies on the way, I became convinced she, like all parents, would want more than this for her kittens. She'd want a more secure, happy lifestyle.

This was a mission that would require research and prayer. I prayed for guidance and wisdom in undertaking this journey. (Ask, and it will be given to you; seek, and you will find; knock, and it will be opened to you. Matthew 7:7)

Internet searches, books about cats, discussions with the local shelters and Humane Associations, and discussions with local veterinarians comprised my early research. I studied the behavior of cats during pregnancy and kitten rearing, pregnancy to term for cats. (The average gestation period for kittens is 60–63 days, in most cases.) I read about the birth process, survival rates, and what to expect as the kittens grew week to week. Noting the best age to trap or handle the kittens, socializing them, and techniques on working with feral kittens to win their trust and acclimate them to the indoor lifestyle were all crucial as we started down this journey together. There was insight and advice on vetting and potential placement of the kittens when the time was right. (We discovered that some local county shelters or Humane Associations had humane feral traps they would loan you to assist with catching feral kittens/cats. Some of them had staff or experienced volunteers who would assist with trapping.)[1]

Throughout her pregnancy, we could keep a closer eye on Josie due to her increased trips to the food area. The afternoon she appeared there having lost the extra weight; we knew her babies had arrived!

It required some sleuth work, but I discovered where Josie had hidden the babies. Tucked away under the skirting around the outside of our mobile home close to her food area was the ideal location. It was possible to check on them there to make sure they were well, but we wouldn't bother Josie's nest.

The day I spotted her cutting across the yard of another mobile home catty-cornered to ours, I realized she had relocated just a few feet away. (Outdoor cats often move their litters to keep them safe and hidden from predators.) She did this 2–3 more times while nursing. We continued to keep an eye on where they were, but never bothered them.

The weeks passed while they grew until the day Josie showed up at her food area with 5 tiny additions in tow. She was cautiously leading the kittens to the food bowls. We'd been feeding her moist kitten food during her pregnancy for nutrition, and now the babies were old enough to eat the kitten food alongside her.

Josie had relocated them one last time back under our home, steps from the food, and we could see where they had pushed a bit of the skirting aside for the kittens to come and go through the gap.

They would play under the skirting, coming out to run and chase one another, but never straying too far from the protection of the side of the home. Sitting on the back stairs a couple feet away, I could watch them play until they accepted me as part of the environment.

Once they reached the age to begin socializing, I brought wand toys and bits of old t-shirt material ripped into long strands to dangle and get their attention. They interacted and batted at the toys. Slowly, I moved closer and closer, eventually being able to reach out and touch them gently. Some kittens responded to this and others did not. For those that allowed us to touch or pet them, it was much easier to catch them and bring them inside. The others required humane traps to catch them and then acclimate them inside to begin socialization.

I gauged Josie's reaction to her kittens coming with me; she never objected. There was an undeniable feeling of betrayal on my part when the time came to remove Josie's kittens. They had reached the age where the constant attention from mama cat naturally waned.

In the natural progression of things, the mama cat's instincts guided her on caring for her kittens, starting before they are born, through the phase of constant care for tiny babies, and when it's time to give them space to develop their independence. I developed an admiration and respect for the devotion mama cats apply to raising their kittens from the early stages to weaning. It's an intense 24/7 job that requires 100% dedication. Once the kittens are weaned, they become more independent, and mamas are less protective. Josie proved this to be true, and through her reactions I felt more confident in doing what I knew was right for the kittens.

Following her first litter, I continued trying to catch Josie to have her spayed and stop the cycle of births. She was too wily to fall for it, despite our trial and error with several types of traps. A cat can become pregnant up to 5 times a year. It's unhealthy, putting considerable strain on their bodies. This is what we were striving to protect her from. Their bodies need a chance to recover after having kittens, to protect her health and the health of any future kittens.

Josie and I worked together through the next few litters of kittens, utilizing the process we'd established. We succeeded in helping the kittens, but my concern for Josie grew with each litter she had. I continued looking for a way to trap her. (There was no help available from our local humane shelter as all of their experienced trappers were buried in the number of kittens from the recent 'kitten season.')

Gregg and I were looking forward to having our first home built, and as the time when it would be completed was drawing closer, I pondered: *What do I do with Josie?*

This was no small dilemma. Josie and I had worked out our system. She had taught me so many things through experience about the care of cats: the cycle of rebirth, and the life of an outdoor cat, trapping ferals, and the importance of spay/neuter. She was my cat mentor, my friend, and I wasn't sure I was ready to give that up.

Would it be fair to her to take her somewhere new where I was not sure I could accommodate her?

The location of the new house was without any provisions to keep Josie and her kittens safe. There was no fencing yet, no enclosed area to protect or shelter them. We didn't know the environment well enough to know what she might face. Josie would be in a precarious position if we transported her to an unfamiliar territory where she would not have the advantages she had in the mobile home court.

Is she better off with me and we'll figure out accommodations? What was the right thing to do? If I leave her here, am I abandoning her? Is it wiser to leave her where she can function?

If she remained here in her neighborhood, we knew she had other people watching over her, feeding her, and letting her live as she was accustomed. She knew where to seek shelter and which homes she could rely on for assistance. She could continue raising her current kittens and continue her routines as she had before. This would still allow me to plan to return and work on trapping her to have her spayed.

Was that realistic? What was the right thing to do?

My heart was torn. Conflicted, I felt like the answer was outside of my reach. So I prayed, asking for God to speak to me. I prayed He would help me understand His guidance clearly and be willing to follow His direction. I didn't want to let my will determine the right course of action for Josie.

My instincts to take her were incredibly strong, and I reasoned this would allow me to keep her safe, trusting that she would adjust to a new environment. She trusted me and I was so uncomfortable about leaving her behind.

I was committed to her and loved her and wanted the best outcome for her. *Shouldn't I be there for her?* This must be God's will as well.

As the days counted down to our scheduled move, catching Josie with her kittens proved to be a challenge. She still avoided the traps, and I couldn't take her young kittens without her, or her without them. It was an impossible situation.

We loaded our last load of belongings into the van, we'd completed the last walk through, and we were ready to head to the new location. Gregg closed the back of the van and sat down in the driver's seat, prepared to head out.

We were still without Josie and the kittens.

My intention was to still catch them that night and take them with us. I'd set an extra-large dog carrier in the side yard, with the door propped open and sat their food bowls inside. (I'd had some luck trapping with this method before.)

At the last moment, I looked to find Josie and her babies inside the dog carrier, all together!

My heart leaped, and I shouted in excitement, "There they are!"

Preparing to jump out, snap the lid shut and bring them with us. *This is what I am meant to do!*

Gregg's voice intervened. "Do you really want to take them now? Where will you put them? Doesn't it make more sense to leave her where you know she'll survive?

Let's go on tonight and we'll come back out for you to trap them."

Understanding the wisdom of what Gregg was saying, I still struggled against my instincts, pushing me to take them now while I had the chance. How could I bear to drive off and leave them all here without knowing their future? I could easily come back and trap them once we had things set up at the new home, right?

Gregg was right. I needed the means to look after her, which would take a little time.

My heart in my throat, we drove away that evening as I sat watching my friend and her little brood all together until they were out of sight. Somewhere in my soul, I knew things would never be the same, but I didn't realize then that it was goodbye.

Over the next few weeks, I made several unsuccessful trips to trap Josie and her babies. Arriving on my first trip, I found the carrier where I'd left it, empty and abandoned. It was clear Josie had moved to another area where she could find shelter and food. She had existed in the park before I'd ever arrived, but this still felt like a terrible betrayal on my part. I'd never succeeded in having her spayed. I struggle with that to this day.

My last memory of Josie is the night I watched them all nestled together inside the dog crate, eating as we drove away.

I wish someone would have convinced me then what a mistake it would've been to pull Josie out of her environment and take her with me to the promise of nothing. It might've eased the guilt and the feeling that I'd betrayed her that I carried for so long.

As I reflect over serving Josie, the pain is still there, yet I hear God's interjections differently in that experience. My heart could have been overpowering the word of God. I'd asked God to show me the truth in my moment of confusion. I believe I let my own heart, distracted by the desire to keep my friend with me, drive my intent to take her. I was allowing my thoughts and desires to convince me it was God's will.

God guided me, telling me what would be best for Josie and her kittens, but it wasn't the outcome I'd been prepared to hear. Those moments of truth that interrupted my thoughts were his voice guiding me to the answer. Gregg said the same words, serving as a megaphone for God's guidance. (For he is our God, and we are the people of his pasture, and the sheep of his hand. Psalm 95:7)

The different lessons God opens us up to as we review memories years later are amazing. The way we view time is much different from how God views time. God was doing exactly what I prayed for even though I did not recognize it. I see now why my plans did not work out. Even though I was not following God's advice, God was working for Josie's good (similar to Bud's journey later in the book).

Perhaps in this case, Josie was here to serve me instead of the other way around?

She opened my heart to the love for God's animals inside, teaching and guiding me toward my true calling. Finally, I learned the importance of not letting the world sway you from how God is guiding you through your intuition.

For he delivers the needy when he calls, the poor and him who has no helper. Psalm 72:12

But do not overlook this one fact, beloved, that with the Lord one day is as a thousand years, and a thousand years as one day. The Lord is not slow to fulfill his promise as some count slowness, but is patient toward you, not wishing that any should perish, but that all should reach repentance. 2 Peter 3:8–9

Molson

God's Miracle Cat

No act of kindness, no matter how small, is ever wasted for God knows your heart and sees it all. —Aesop

From the first moment I saw him through the back door, it was clear something was wrong. There were no visible signs of injury or abuse, nothing obvious to point to; it was more his overall aura. Something wasn't right about the lanky, orange tabby stretched across the large, flat rock in our backyard.

His face looked up directly toward the sun with a content look (it's a cat thing) as he lay basking in the warmth. I watched as he yawned, stretched his long legs out, then rolled over onto his side and relaxed again.

He was rail thin and fragile looking, with no shine or luster to his faded orange coat. (Though I could see the former splendor and color he once exhibited.) I called him Molson after Molson Golden brand beer, as a tribute to another rescue cat I had once known. He was an adult cat, young judging from his size and ease of movement. Molson gave off gentle energy, a quiet, laid-back manner, allowing me to approach him when I stepped outside for a closer look. He looked up at me slowly, and I saw he had very kind eyes, but they were tired looking and pale. His face looked gaunt, not the more giant head, or full cheeks of most adult males. On a hunch, I checked the color of his gums, finding they were also pale (anemia).

I'd seen this before amidst other cats in this neighborhood. His combined symptoms all pointed to one illness: Leukemia (FeLV).

Feline leukemia is a retrovirus easily transmitted among cats. Symptoms in an infected cat can include anemia, paleness of the skin, tongue, gums, and mucous membranes surrounding the eye, weight loss, rough coat, loss of appetite, vomiting, diarrhea, respiratory distress, and a list of additional issues. There is no cure for FeLV, but there are treatments to boost the immune system for infected cats.[2]

Prevention is the best course of action and can be achieved by a series of vaccinations for kittens that are common and often taken at the same time as the FVRCP series. (FVRCP is a combination vaccination that protects against multiple diseases that kittens are susceptible to.)

The one caveat to consider is that once a feline has had a FeLV injection, they may test positive for the infection itself based on the antibodies in its bloodstream. This is a risk to stray or rescue cats whose history is unknown. In these cases, the recommendation is generally to do a series of tests a few months apart to determine if the positive result is vaccine related, or true infection.[3]

We'd encountered enough cases of FeLV previously to recognize that Molson's visible symptoms indicated he had an advanced set of complications from the virus. So many of the outdoor cats from this neighborhood were FIV + or FeLV.

Knowing there is no cure, there was little we could do other than to make him comfortable and provide palliative care. We could ensure he was looked after and that his time left here on Earth would be spent with us as comfortably as we could make it. We were determined to help this sweet soul.

It was hard to understand how such a wonderful boy would be able to endure this illness on his own, as we had found him.

How did he end up outside on his own? Had he been abandoned once he was diagnosed? Had he grown up here in the outside colony, contracted it, or been born with it as a kitten? What has his life been like up to now?

We would never learn his history, but we prayed daily for God to guide us through his care and show us the right choices to make on his behalf. We prayed God would grant us the wisdom to recognize when the time was right to let him go so he did not suffer.

At first, we struggled with the dilemma of knowing Molson was ill and letting him remain outdoors. There was the risk of exposure to the other neighborhood cats to consider. The dangers all outdoor cats faced, the possibility he could go off on his own when his time arrived, and we would never know. His love of being outdoors and his tendency not to wander too far from our yard gave us some peace. The threat of one sick cat introducing and contaminating the neighborhood here was long past. Our resolution to give Molson a great life while we had him firmly in our hearts, we maintained the lifestyle he had when we met him, the lifestyle he loved.

As the summer went on, Molson was content to call our yard his own. Each day I'd look out to find him sunning on his favorite rock, bathing his front paws, and closing his eyes in contentment. This boy didn't ask much from life and seemed content with what he'd found. Warm sun, food, water, and being loved wasn't such a bad lifestyle. When the days proved to be too warm for him, he would wander in through the backdoor to visit with us and perhaps lay in some air conditioning for a while. (We previously cared for FeLV-positive cats within our own cat population with no issues. Given the proper precautions and a stable environment, we'd never had a case of contamination.)

We were blessed to spend the late spring into summer in Molson's company. He was such a gentle soul it was easy to be in his presence, and equally easy to care for and love him. He blended into our 'pack' so well that we'd tend to forget our time with him was limited.

When the fall gave way to the colder temperatures of the oncoming winter, Molson disappeared. He was no longer in the backyard. I didn't see him at all. Perhaps the warm flat rock, so enticing in the summer, no longer held the same promise of warmth in winter. Still, with the plentiful food dish and the warmth available underneath mobile homes in the park, he would never choose to walk away. Something had happened.

There had been no question that Molson's time left here on Earth was short from the day we'd met. He was undeniably ill, to an advanced degree. I feared that his infection had advanced to the stage that he'd chosen to wander off and die peacefully on his own. We'd acknowledged this possibility with the decision to let him continue outdoors, but it didn't lessen the fear or pain of not knowing.

After the second day he'd failed to return, his disappearance launched us into a search of the immediate area. We followed his usual route and checked under the nearby mobile homes, hoping to find him or some sign of him. If he were hurt or faltering and I could find him, I'd bring him home where he could be safe. If we found him passed, then at least we could get him home for burial.

After we'd exhausted every avenue to find him with no results, we returned defeated. I cried at the loss of my friend, thinking the natural conclusion was that Molson's time had come, and he had chosen to go off on his own for his last moments. There might never be a resolution or the knowledge of his end for us, so I tried to accept that it was done, and acknowledge he'd chosen how he wanted to go.

I prayed God was with him, keeping him in His arms whatever his current circumstance. I prayed God would return him to us if it were His will, but if not, that He please protect Molson from any pain, harm, or fear.

The process of cat and kitten rescue continued as I reached out to those in need. The holiday season was in full swing. In addition to the hustle and bustle of the season, it's also a busy and exciting time in rescue as many families choose to adopt a new pet into their families during the season. Additionally, many outdoor feral cats also needed extra care and attention to keep them safe and comfortable during the cold months.

Among all this, occasionally I glanced over to where the large, flat rock still lay in the yard and reminisced about Molson.

This winter brought some windy, cold days and more snow than I could recall seeing since we'd been in Tennessee. As we approached New Year's Eve, a solid blanket of snow was on the ground. My mother was in town visiting, and Gregg was also home this year. (As a musician, this is generally one of the busiest nights for him.) So, we planned to stay in and celebrate the new year at home.

To this day, I can't honestly say what I was doing when I heard it.

There was a persistent but weak whining coming from outside the front door. I listened and strained to see if I'd really heard this, trying to identify what it might be. By the second occurrence, I recognized the strained sounds of a gargled meow. I threw open the front door, expecting to see one of our visiting cats, perhaps a new feline in need in the neighborhood. When I saw him, I gasped!

There, amid the blowing snow and cold, was Molson! With his cold paws pressed against the screen door, meowing in a tired, raspy voice was our Molson! I called for Gregg to come.

This was shocking. Unsure what to believe, we wasted no time in bringing him in from the cold.

This poor baby was terribly thin, freezing with snow clinging halfway up his legs, and completely covering his paws. One look at him and we could see he was now totally blind. He stared blankly at the door, knowing this was the way back inside but not seeing it. Molson tilted his head at my voice, calling his name as I snatched him up to come inside. He was following the sound of my voice with his head. Still, his little eyes had a whitish cast, and he wasn't focusing on anything, only listening to find his bearings. He was emaciated and weak and collapsed slightly in my arms once he realized he was safe. He was home.

We hurried to get him wrapped in a warming blanket with a heating pad. Holding him closely, I shared my body heat with him and spoke to him in soothing, calm tones, reassuring him.

Tucking him into a soft bed, we hand fed him some chicken we'd had for dinner. He ate greedily, anxious for the food to fill his belly. We rationed our feeding, offering him only the amount he could easily digest in a series of small feedings over the next couple of hours.

Where had he been all this time, and how had he found his way back to us now? How had this sweet, gentle boy, felled by leukemia, been gone so long, yet survived and miraculously found his way back home, totally blind?

Had he gotten stuck in a tool shed somewhere? Accidentally gotten into the back of a work truck and transported somewhere else? Had someone else found him and taken him in until they realized he was sick, or they'd moved off (like so many do in the mobile home parks)? The scenarios ran through our heads as we all tried our best to make some sense of what had happened here tonight.

We marveled at what he must've been through, what he had overcome and faced finding his way home to us. God had honored our requests to hold and keep Molson safe and blessed us further by returning him to us to spend his final hours with the family that loved him. It was a miracle! (Ask, and it will be given to you; seek, and you will find; knock, and it will be opened to you. For everyone who asks receives, and the one who seeks finds, and to the one who knocks it will be opened. Matthew 7:7–8) We kept him warm and comfortable and close by us for companionship, so amazed and happy he had made it back. He had dozed off in his warm bed, with his belly full, finally warm and safe.

Molson awakened shortly after that, spasming and struggling to breathe. Raspy breaths were audible, taking all the energy he had to pull air in and exhale. I held him against me, whispering to him and hugging him.

Knowing now we were in the final stages of the epic battle for his life; we decided to make the last desperate attempt to reach the emergency vet to see if there was something we could do to ease his pain. We knew we wouldn't win the battle, but could we ease his struggle in passing? We took off in the snow, Molson in my arms in our last desperate attempt. He was so still that I held my hand on his chest to ensure I could feel him breathing.

Somewhere around halfway to the vet, Molson released his last tethered breath (death rattle) and passed on. I sat in shock, telling Gregg with as much voice as I could muster, that he was gone.

Looking back, I wonder if Molson was really in tune with what was happening at the moment. I believe he felt my arms around him and the love and warmth we felt for him. I hope he felt comforted and felt the love with which we handed him from our arms to God.

I genuinely believe it was one cat's determination to return home, where he knew he was loved, to spend his last moments on earth. God granted Molson the wishes of his heart by guiding him on this journey home so he would finish his story with those who loved him and wanted to be there to help him when he needed it most.

Sometimes, I still imagine what his journey might've been like, battling the cold in his vulnerable, weak state, emaciated, and blind but determined to make it home. I had prayed for God to keep him safe in His protection and to block any pain from touching him, even when we remained in the dark about what had happened. God honored that prayer in such a way we could never have imagined. He brought him home to say goodbye.

We pray God will use us in His service for the good of His animals in need. And while we imagine what that typical happy ending will look like, God is at work with a much more expansive parameter of what is "happiness" and "comfort." We might've hoped for a different ending, but God saw into Molson's heart and chose what was important to bring happiness to him.

In the end, God granted us an unusual joy by allowing us to be a part of Molson's last moments on Earth, to know his final chapter and not be left wondering what had happened to him, and mostly the honor of knowing Molson considered us his home. He knew he was loved, that he mattered, and will remain in our hearts until we see him again.

Sure, in my mind, joy would have looked like Molson never disappearing. Still, this ministry has taught me to remain open to God's redefined wonder of unusual joy.

God blessed us to be there to send Molson to Him with love, from the arms of his family on Earth to the beautiful arms of God and the Kingdom of Heaven.

I celebrate these moments and how they sustain me professionally and personally as I serve.

> May the God of hope fill you with all joy and peace in believing, so that by the power of the Holy Spirit you may abound in hope. Romans 15:13

> So also you have sorrow now, but I will see you again, and your hearts will rejoice, and no one will take away your joy from you. John 16:22

Tip

My Soul Tie

Animals know how to speak to those who know how to listen. —Unknown

Arriving home after work early one evening, I climbed out of the car and something caught my eye from the side. I turned to find a tiny tuxedo kitten running in my direction as fast as his little legs would carry him. No mistake, he was heading right for me, meowing as loud as he could manage. And so, as simple as that, I reached down, opened my hand, and he ran right into it. I scooped him up, holding him close; I looked around to see if anyone or anything was chasing him, but no. No one was looking around for a lost kitten, either. He was out here on his own.

It was not unusual to find stray cats in the mobile home park where we were living. It *was* unusual to have one come charging out of nowhere directly at me!

Exactly how he'd come to be there or how long he had been waiting for someone to help him remains a mystery. Although the determination with which he was running, and the fact that the entire bridge of his nose had been colored in with permanent black marker, was a good indication he'd escaped from the home up the road to the right. There was a trailer with a notorious young child left unsupervised who seemed to be an expert at 'finding' these small animals. We had intervened on a couple of other occasions to assist other poor animals that had fallen victim to his 'care.' (The prevailing theory was he found these babies from feral groups in the trailer park and took them home.)

Regardless of where this baby came from, he had been desperate to escape. Now that he was here, he would remain safe. We went into the house together, where he settled into a large, cozy box set up with soft blankets and toys, and a couple of other tiny kittens from the neighborhood we were helping. It is always amazing how far a little comfort, food, and a feeling of safety can go. The kitten continued to meow a bit (I believe he was telling his story). He settled in to nap, sleeping that deep, content sleep animals enjoy when they know they are genuinely safe and their souls achieve peace.

His first vet checkup confirmed he was a male, in good health despite the ink coloring his nose. A pretty tuxedo kitten with bright green eyes, and one bright white tip on the end of his tail. When the veterinarian commented on the bright white tip on an otherwise dark black tail, I instantly knew his name: Tip.

Tip settled in quickly to this new environment and proved to be an extremely precocious kitten. He was intelligent and outgoing, with a mind of his own. He had confidence beyond his young age and was not afraid to try anything that looked interesting, tasty, or fun! Over the next few weeks, Tip and our other kittens (including his new best friend Spot, a male yellow tabby kitten) spent their time playing and growing, finding unending things to investigate. They were young and had time to enjoy just being kittens together, and we enjoyed them.

In rescue, it never hurts to tell the story of each kitten early, enhancing their biography with the exciting quirks, personality traits, and pictures that showcase them. Most adopters love to follow the stories and watch them grow until the day they can take them home! So, I featured them on our adoption sites.

In the back of my mind, I knew I would love to keep Tip, adding him to our small, permanent group of pets. He and I had built a strong bond when I'd picked him up and brought him inside. But a more reasonable choice (the 'rescuer code') would be to find him a home where he could be more than one of many in rescue, where he could be someone's special cat. I prayed for guidance and for God to lead my heart to do what was best for Tip overall.

The weeks passed quickly, and the kittens had been vetted and grown old enough to settle into permanent loving homes. Jane, a colleague from work, had expressed interest in adopting a kitten, and she particularly liked how I had described Tip. I was excited for him—this could be his home! It would be great for me as well to keep tabs on Tip from time to time. His buddy Spot had recently been adopted by a work colleague of my mother's, so Tip was on his own at this point.

When Jane met the kittens, she was drawn to a small, charming, but timid calico and struggled with the choice between the two kittens. (Another example of cats choosing their people.) I shared with her some of the many benefits of adopting two kittens together (It's always an advantage for kittens to be adopted in pairs: for companionship, to learn from one another, and it helps to ease the stress of adjusting to a new home.) Gregg also pointed out the advantages of adopting two kittens together, and the deal was made.

While we settled the kittens into the carrier and prepared them for their journey to a new home, I was simultaneously elated for Tip, but also a little sad. Selfishly, I wanted the best for Tip, but I loved him at the same time and would miss our bond. I reminded myself that it would be extremely hard to say goodbye and I would miss him, but the fundamental goal of rescue is always to do what is best for the cats. He was on his way to his new home with the bonus of being adopted by someone I knew and trusted. I offered a prayer on their behalf for the future, exhaled, and set my intentions on positive, encouraging energy focused on their new beginning! Knowing the importance of how cats pick up on the energy around them and will respond, it was imperative I send them off with hope and love to guide them.

So off they went on their new journey.

At that point, my resolve let go and I was flooded with a mixed bag of joy, excitement, sadness, and loss all at once. I went into the other room where my husband was to tell him the news that they were on their way home. That's when I was overcome with tears. (It's always hard to watch an animal you've nurtured and loved leave; I cry each time.) But this was something different. The intensity was so pronounced I have rarely felt it so quickly with another cat.

Gregg and I talked; he hugged me as I cried. I confessed I had hoped it would work out for us to keep Tip. I had sincerely bonded with him and loved him. The feeling that it would've been a selfish decision on my part is why I had resigned to let Tip go. We talked about how he had gone to a good home with a good person. I would be grateful for that and ask God to heal my heart.

I set my mind to go about my day. Time to close that chapter.

Less than an hour later, there was a knock at the front door. It surprised me to find Jane again holding the kitten carrier in her hand. She came in with Tip in the carrier and began telling me the story of why she felt she needed to bring him back to us.

They had heard a scuffling sound coming from the carrier. And when they peeked in to check it out, they were just in time to witness Tip slapping the little calico on the head and intimidating her into the corner of the carrier!

We were both surprised. This was odd, as Tip had never displayed aggression toward other kittens before. These two had been raised together; playing together countless times, and went into the carrier together with no issues. It could have been the stress of being in the carrier or the change in environment. I believe Tip felt our bond and knew he was home. He didn't want to leave it; we had miles to go together. This was his refusal to leave. Ultimately, the couple was uncomfortable trying to adopt them together. So, there was Tip in the carrier with them asking if they could return Tip?

I went through a second rush of emotions that day. In the moment, I stood there surprised, elated, and sad for Tip all at once. But I also knew the minute Tip was back inside the house, I would not let him go again. This was our second chance, and our bond was too strong to let him go again willingly. I also knew this was no coincidence.

He was placed into my life in such a deliberate and unique way; he was meant to be here. I genuinely believe he knew it, too. God had sent him with a purpose, and I had felt it, but failed to recognize the significance of God's gift. I had felt pulled by the 'right thing to do' as the world defined it, and almost missed out on one of the best friends of my life. (I imagine God laughing as He sent Tip kitten back and said "here!")

Tip was quite the presence in our home for 16+ years. He was a 'cat's cat' among our entire clowder. (At one point we were up to 10 permanent resident cats.) He was like the big brother, keeping the peace and promoting harmony among the other cats by setting an example. Tip ruled with an iron paw inside a velvet fur glove.

He remained feisty at times, stubborn to be sure, and never afraid to express himself with me and the other human members of the family. Sometimes, he would tire of my constant attention, whether affection, or a game we were playing together. Sometimes it would be the phrases I would say to tease him or a pet name I'd call him in a sing-song voice. (Tip even inspired the writing of several 'jingles' around the house, and a couple of full-length songs that were recorded as a part of the repertoire of our original blues band and released internationally.)

Each time, his eyes would narrow, he would look me directly in the face, ears back, and huff out an exasperated breath. He would either jump to his feet and leave or keep the look going and slowly raise a front paw back as if to dare me to keep it up. We had our own language together. My husband would laugh at us, saying he'd never seen anyone argue as much as we did, walk away mad, but make up two minutes later. And Heaven help anyone who stepped in the middle.

There is no doubt looking back now. It's quite clear that this precocious, feisty, loyal kitten was meant to be one of my dearest friends. God sent him to my life, and even when I'd almost given him away, God had reinforced what I had missed in interpreting His answer to my prayers. He really did have me at hello, and ours was a unique relationship that I cherish to this day.

We had over 16 years with Tip, that seemed to fly by. In his later years, we fought a valiant battle alongside him against thyroid disease. We did all we could for him, including Radioactive Iodine (I-131) therapy for feline hyperthyroidism (which boasts a 95–98% success rate for most cats after one treatment, prolonging their lives by 4–5 years on average.) It was a complicated process for Tip. Even the separation we endured while he was in treatment with the vet for 2–3 days was rough on us all. We'd never been separated since the day he'd been returned by my work associate so many years before.

And as heart-wrenching as it is to have lost him so soon, it was the bond we shared and the language we spoke together that guided me in the end to let him go when he needed to.

The day we were able to pick him up from the treatment, the technician entered the room with his carrier, and a very confused, frightened cat looked out from it. I hated that. But when his eyes landed on us there in the exam room, the relief was visible on his face.

Despite all the warnings in the literature and by his treating veterinarian's office to avoid close contact with Tip right after this treatment (low levels of radiation) the minute we arrived home, he was out of the carrier and into my lap. That night, he slept on the side of my pillow as he'd always done. It just felt right to have him home.

I was just confident that the worst was now over. Tip was home, the treatments over, and all that was left was to heal. But it became evident quickly that Tip didn't show the progress we'd expected. His symptoms and evidence of illness were advancing.

We were doing everything we could to manage the decline. He was going to be given IV fluids over the next few days to prevent nausea. We needed to give him a springboard to keep him on the healing path.

In the days that followed, despite all we tried, Tip became lethargic, and mostly slept or hid in the closet for peace and quiet.

I prayed. The prayers started with pleas to God to provide the healing and life energy back that was once Tip. I missed my feisty boy and knew we weren't going to win this fight without the Lord's help.

My prayers changed as I witnessed the light dimming in Tip's eyes and his energy and love of life slipping away. I gave up praying for the outcome I wanted, and I asked the Lord to spare him any further pain and discomfort. It was more important now to pray for what Tip wanted. I prayed for the strength to know when the time was here to let him go, and for the strength to do it.

The answer came the following day as I was preparing to take him to the vet for his IV treatment. It was hard, and he hated it, I knew. I did too. I was ready to load him up and go, but I looked over to see him curled up, his face buried in the back corner of his carrier.

This was not Tip.

Tip never went willingly into a carrier and he indeed never turned his back on the door and all that was going on around him.

Tip's eyes caught mine as I peered inside, and my heart sank. I knew in an instant he'd had enough. He just couldn't bear another trip, another IV needle, another day feeling this way. Tip's soul was speaking to me loud and clear, and his eyes pleaded with me to let him go. I recall that moment so clearly, even to this day.

"Okay Tippy," I told him.

"I'll miss you terribly. I love you, I can let you go, this is goodbye, my friend."

Accepting that Tip had fought as long as he could, and that the time had come to release him, I prayed again. This time for God to welcome Tip into His arms and reward his soul, and to give me the strength I knew I needed to get through this one hour at a time.

The world instantly took on a surreal quality, as if I was observing everything unfolding from outside my body to protect myself from what was coming. I was projecting myself into the scene, doing what was needed, but from a safe distance. My energy was protecting me from feeling the intensity of the pain I was fending off to help me make it through. From this strangely protected state, I texted my vet immediately to let them know Tip was coming today, but for a different purpose.

Still wrapped in a sense that I was observing this reality outside myself, I called Gregg at work. It was then, when I heard his voice, that the 'protective' bubble burst. Suddenly grounded again in reality and forced to face what was happening. As hard as I tried to speak, I was so overcome that I cried so violently that I struggled to find my voice to tell him what was happening. I managed to squeak out the words Tip, and I'm not sure what else, but he knew.

"I'm coming home." he told me. "Stay there until I get there and we'll go."

There were other words of comfort, but my mind doesn't recall them.

I turned to Tip and began our private goodbye while we were alone and I could share with him how much he meant to me. After all the times we'd shared over the years, I confided to him I didn't know how to do this or say goodbye. Our hearts were there together, wide open in grief together knowing this was our final hour.

We entered the bereavement room at the veterinarian's office prepared to release Tip. He had lived a good life and was greatly loved; we were confident he knew it. My heart was shattered, and I cried. I concentrated on one breath after the other while time seemed to stand still.

I was determined to send a tip off to God with dignity and grace, so their reunion would be joyous and wonderful.

Preparations made, I held my precious friend and whispered words of love and encouragement in his ear. (Positive energy to send him on his journey.) I knew he would forgive my sadness at this moment of goodbye. I had shared my private goodbye with Tip at home before the journey, but in the moments before he left, I told him again how loved and cherished he was, how much he had added to our lives.

The moments leading up to his release were the worst. I prayed, asking the Lord to send me a sign, any type of reassurance that Tip was home in His arms, and safe.

The moment arrived, and the instant Tip was free, I watched his soul's essence rise. I saw his energy leave his body and rise up to Heaven. It was beautiful and surreal, and he was gone. In that instant, his soul was at rest; I stopped crying. I felt the peace wash over me and knew that he was with God.

I thanked God for the friendship he'd sent me years before.

On a couple of occasions in the following year, Tip's essence came a couple more times to visit. Unexpectedly, he would be in a familiar pose, in a favorite place, or performing a familiar task. It was always just a glance, a moment of familiarity and comfort. More than the visual, I felt his energy, felt his presence, then he was gone. It was a reminder of the bond we shared, and a loving, warm feeling in my heart that brought a smile.

God was delivering His comfort and reassurance still to heal my heart.

Through serving Tip, it was affirmed in me that any soul that you love and connect with on earth remains with you after they leave the earthly plane. Our relationships and bonds formed with our pets stretch beyond space and time as we know it through soul-ties. Animals are true expressions of God's love in their ability to give love unconditionally. In many cases, even after a bad experience with mankind, they will forgive and love again. Our earthly understanding of love is limited to our experiences here until we are able to reunite with these souls and return to the pure energy of God's love.

Noted Author, Artist, and Speaker Hans Wilhelm describes the relationship of souls in his book/video series "Life Explained" (LIFEexplained.com). He describes the relationship by suggesting that because God is the eternal Creator of all lifeforms and loves all his children. In His realm of pure love, animals are also created with an ethereal body because they are continuously animated by God. He believes that out of pure love many of the ethereal life forms of the animal kingdoms incarnated here on Earth to help us find our way back home to God. This was a total act of selfless love, part of the act of pure love that consists of the joy to serve.

While the reason for Tip's essence returning to me on those mystical visits has still not made itself known to me, it does not make the occurrences any less impactful or meaningful. It was enough for me to simply experience him and know he is still connected to my heart.

Sometimes we as Christians can simply ignore these mystical moments because of potential subconscious negative stigmas. However, I would encourage you to embrace them, for within them are true blessings.

God heals with energy and love and not knowing the how, or why does not make the blessing any less powerful.

> ...and the sweetness of a friend comes from his earnest counsel Proverbs 27:9

> Who teaches us more than the beasts of the earth and makes us wiser than the birds of the heavens? Job 35:11

Bud

A Tiger's Heart

Not all of us can do great things. But we can do small things with great love. —Mother Teresa

He was a big ole gray tabby, an adult tomcat from the neighborhood, with a self-assured stride. The natural swagger in his step was evidence of the total confidence he possessed. A street tough to be sure, and the king of all he surveyed. In his own mind, he was a fierce tiger, and this was *his* neighborhood, his world. (We would come to know later his tough exterior hid a loving nature. More on that to come...)

His most prominent feature was his large incisors hanging down from his mouth just a little too far below his lips.

They poked out on either side so that they were visible even when his mouth was closed. They resembled fangs, giving him the look of a vampire. A very dashing vampire, to be sure.

His rugged good looks and easy charm were unmistakable. He resembled his ancestral line of the tiger, just a few sizes smaller to fit into the modern life of a domestic cat. He had beautiful cream and tan marbling throughout his dark gray fur with a concentration of these lighter colors on part of his lower belly, his muzzle, and the subtle pattern of rings along the top of his tail.

His head resembled a 'champagne glass' shaped triangle, widening through his cheeks to the broadest part of his forehead where his perfectly triangular ears sat. Big, intelligent, green eyes looked out from the center of his face just above the bridge of his nose, which ended in the telltale pink nose leather at the end (Real men wear pink, you know). His nose was surrounded on both sides with long, white whiskers on both cheeks. I called him Bud.

Bud had the perfect life with just one exception: he was homeless.

We chanced to meet one evening when he appeared across the ravine at the back of our house. He was clearly on his way over to the feeding station I maintained near the back steps in a quiet part of our yard. Approaching with a smooth, confident stride, he slowed just a tad to make a conservative approach after he spotted me sitting there on the steps observing. He continued his stride to the food more cautiously than before.

Raising his head to look me in the eye, he assessed the situation. I glanced away and didn't move, seemingly disinterested. Seeing there was no imminent attack awaiting him, he dropped his head to eat, glancing at me from time to time to monitor my movements.

The evenings that followed unfolded similarly. Topping off the feeding station with fresh water and food, I would take my seat and wait on the back stoop for Bud to make his appearance. It was poetic, watching his handsome face appear across the ravine, his neck stretched up slightly, looking over to survey the situation. Seeing no immediate obstacles, he would arch gracefully, jump the ravine, and land with a soft thud on the grass. Ambling over, like a tiger to his prey, he would cast a perfunctory glance at me, round the corner of the steps, and approach. He was watchful at first, as I would sit there and just be present with him. As the first few encounters gave way to a routine, the trust between us grew.

I would speak to Bud in a conversational tone about his day, asking what he'd spent his afternoon doing, or what he thought of the dinner selection that evening. We would chat and sit together, watching the sun go down and the moon rise until Bud needed to be on his way. Ours was a gentle friendship based on trust and respect. Neither of us made demands. We were just meeting for our evening chats.

As a musician, it was so natural for melodies to come to me as we sat together out in the evening air. I would sing to him using his name in the songs and blinking to him gently when our eyes met. (A technique borrowed from the nonverbal interactions of cats together is to avoid direct eye contact or staring, seen as confrontational.) Blinking while in the presence of another cat symbolizes non-confrontational behavior, it communicates comfort and trusting enough in their presence to close your eyes. When you receive a blink back, the trust is mutual.

Bud seemed to appreciate the melodies and had tolerated my reaching out to him. He rewarded me with a nose tap or sniff. From there, head pats and very gentle ear rubs became acceptable and earned a soft approving purr.

As our friendship continued to blossom, we would follow the same routine together. It was a very relaxing and centering experience for me just being together and sharing our energy in the calm surroundings. One evening, as Bud approached the steps, rather than sitting near me on the stoop he jumped up and reached out to pat my leg tentatively, with his paw (a sign of friendship) then settled in, placing his head on my lap to rest. This was quite an honor and a testament to our friendship. I knew at that moment this fierce tiger's heart was as big as his fierce fangs. Bud loved me.

It was difficult, but I resisted the urge to stand up and dance, to hug him, and celebrate this bond we'd created! That was my nature, not that of my cat friend, so I dared not jump up just as he had settled in. (Most cat lovers will suffer great hardships like thirst or legs that go to sleep rather than disturb a sleeping cat.) I sat there holding Bud and singing to him, feeling the joy of the milestone we had crossed.

What an amazing feeling to create your own successful communication with another species and to develop it to such a bond of love and trust absent a common verbal language. Bud and I had learned how to speak the language of love.

People in rescue commonly believe that you can't befriend a wild or feral cat after a certain age. (Generally, 4–6 months.) After two months, age, gender, genetics, and life experience of the cat play an important role in determining the difficulty involved. Each cat has their own persona. In truth, predictions of the time needed to tame an older cat are hard to make when all these variables come into play. The idea is widely held, but I never believed it, and Bud was my proof.

The truth is that every rescue, every situation, is different. There is no hard and fast rule that holds true in every case. These types of comments serve better if we regard them as guidelines and not facts.

The progression of our friendship continued to bring new things. Bud explored life inside the house with us. He was adapting beautifully and enjoyed things like air conditioning and the comfy sofa. (Bud developed an adorable habit of snuggling up on my husband's neck to nap with him.) He was happy being with us and enjoying the attention we showered on him, but he was not quite ready to commit to being an indoor-only cat.

He still loved the freedom of wandering through the grass and patrolling his neighborhood. Giving up the wild tiger within, Bud was content to come inside when it suited him, and leave when he was ready. So we respected his terms, while we were aware of the dangers and the risks of the outside lifestyle. We were not entirely at ease with Bud's desire to remain outside; however, we understood it, and we honored it.

Mobile home parks tend to have large outdoor cat populations. Their former owners have abandoned some, some the result of generations of cats left unaltered in reproducing colonies, with a few thrown in here and there who live with residents within the park but are allowed to roam freely.

During the warm months, they seek shade and shelter under the trees or between the homes. In the cold months, they seek warmth and protection by settling underneath the skirting of the homes, drawing warmth from the water pipes that heat through the floors.

This begins the cycle of cats having more cats and so on. The cycle is never-ending if left unchecked. Among the residents, there are usually a few homes that will put food out to help the cats, but the cats will far outnumber the amount of food made available over time. These colonies of cats must learn to survive on their own and the populations grow exponentially, increasing the shortages of food and shelter; communicable disease takes over. This contributes heavily to the spread of FIV+ among the cat colonies due to fighting. (Cats, by nature, are incredibly territorial; having to compete for shelter, food, and mates during the season only intensifies these instincts.) An unspayed female at or over 4 months of age can produce approximately three to five litters of kittens per season, each containing up to 12 kittens. (This is a general figure so the actual numbers can vary when the reproduction season begins early or lasts longer into the year.)

Many communities these days also offer low-cost or discounted spay/neuter services to pet owners and rescues alike. Check with your local SPCA or Humane Association and online social media.

Bud had come to us from this environment, and even now, with the advantages of vet care and the safety of indoor life with a family that loved him, it was hard for him to abandon the lifestyle he'd adapted to. (We never knew Bud's origins in the neighborhood, only that it seemed he'd found us not long after finding himself there, based on his health condition and ability to trust humans.)

One evening, Bud showed up as part of our usual dinner ritual, crossed the ravine, and padded across the backyard toward the food station, but this time was different: he had someone with him! Falling right into step behind him was what looked like a miniature version of him. She was a tiny, gray tabby with large eyes and the wider forehead of a kitten, no more than 3–4 months old. The kitten was a beautiful little thing with a perky behind that turned slightly up at the end, and no tail. She was a Manx! (The Manx breed of cat is defined by a mutation that shortens the tail. A variety of tail lengths are seen, from normal to taillessness, but it is tailless or extremely short-tailed cats that are characteristic of the breed.) By all appearances, Bud had taken this young kitten under his wing to show her the ropes.

We had to wonder about their association. You don't often hear of a grown male cat adopting a kitten to care for, especially among outdoor cats. She was wary, as Bud had been at our first meeting, but displayed absolute trust in Bud, and followed him up to the feeding area. The resemblance to Bud was so strong that we appropriately named her Bud Light. We have never learned how these two came to be together. Bud Light became a much-loved member of our adopted family and has her own story within our Doodlebug Manor crew.

Over time, Bud became accustomed to spending more of his time inside with us and had settled into a happy routine with our other cats for the most part.

Meanwhile, we continued to take in wayward cats and kittens to rescue. One such cat we'd taken in was another large male who was abandoned in the park. He arrived one day across the ravine much like Bud, but with the wounds and scratches to prove he'd been trying to adapt and survive in an environment he knew nothing about. We named this newcomer Cow as he was a van tabby, primarily white with black spots and patches, a solid black tail, and a large black patch that spilled over the top of his head resembling a rather bad toupee. He was a people-friendly cat and seemed at ease with most of our cats as well. The exception to this amicable arrangement was Bud.

Judging from the eruption of hissing, swatting, and body language that promised to end in all-out warfare when they first spotted each other, we surmised that Cow and Bud had been archenemies from the neighborhood. This would not be easy to negotiate with both cats taking up at least part-time residence within the house. We considered them both part of our family, but for each of them, the existence of the other cat inside crossed acceptable boundaries. We were careful to ensure that when one cat was in the other was out. This proved difficult to manage and was an uncomfortable solution for all of us.

A cause for additional concern was Bud's recent diagnosis as FIV+ (Feline immunodeficiency virus) at his vet appointment. This was when the knowledge of FIV in cats was limited at best. The typical response among veterinarians, and the public alike, was to euthanize FIV+ cats to prevent the spread of the disease, and to prevent suffering on the part of the feline. Very little was known about the long-term effects or transmission from one feline to another, but those more educated about the disease realized it was not necessarily a death sentence.

When the results from Cow's veterinary visit came back shortly thereafter with the same diagnosis, we weren't surprised (there is a strong likelihood that through fighting, one had passed on the virus to the other) but were disappointed for both boys.[4]

We had worked with FIV+ cats previously in a stable group of cats where there was little threat of the other felines being infected. We had consulted closely with a couple veterinarians to incorporate a holistic treatment routine into their regular healthcare maintenance to boost immune response and lessen any symptoms. The existence of FIV presented us with a couple of dilemmas:

First, the aggression and animosity that existed between the two boys meant that their coexistence in the same home would put both themselves and the other family cats at risk. This was out of the question.

Second, allowing an FIV cat to run outside among other cats presented the threat of contamination and further spread of the disease, putting the outdoor cat population at risk. This would be irresponsible. This was also out of the question.

We loved both cats and wanted to see the best outcome for both. There were several questions and considerations to work through, but no discernable answer.

I alone couldn't find my way to the right answer here, despite my yearning to do right by both cats. I prayed God would guide me and listened for His word. (But Jesus looked at them and said, "With man this is impossible, but with God all things are possible." Matthew 19:26) Shortly thereafter, the solution arrived in the form of a visit from my mother.

My mother had long adored animals, and they her. While growing up, it was common to observe the pets in our home naturally gravitating to her. As we mentioned in previous chapters, my mother had a heart for animals, a loving spirit, and a graceful, easy manner with them that drew them in.

It didn't take long for Cow to succumb to this magnetism. An instant bond between them resulted in Cow's new home! We were thrilled at the outcome God had provided. It proved to be a blessing for Cow and my mother.

Not long after Cow had settled into his new life, our opportunity to purchase our first home had arrived, and we began the moving preparations. It was an exciting new beginning, but along with it came some concerns about how all the cats would adapt to a new environment, given their territorial nature. Our original concerns regarding Bud were back in the forefront again.

Bud's love of the outdoors had not diminished, but it would be a considerable risk to introduce him to a new environment.

Would he adjust to a new neighborhood that was not his old stomping ground where he was 'King'? How would he adapt to an indoor-only lifestyle?

Our best option was to see if Bud would adjust to indoor living full time and try to make some accommodations in the new yard to provide him the necessary outdoor time and to keep him safe and content.

The move went well; the house was newly built, so there were no former occupant scents for the pets to contend with. The cats were a little tense the first few weeks, but settled in well.

At first, Bud went out on accompanied visits in the backyard to enable him to learn the area. However, the continual construction noise from the other homes being built disturbed him. There was a small band of trees in our backyard with a new dog house nestled nearby for Bud to find comfort within his new yard. Unfortunately, it offered little solace. This just wasn't Bud's territory, and he struggled to adjust. I felt the struggle he was facing.

One early evening Bud strayed from his outdoor visit in the yard to go exploring. One minute he was there; then suddenly gone. Hours of calling, searching, and trying to recover my big, independent boy yielded nothing. As days turned into weeks with no word, no sightings, and no responses to my attempts to find him, I slowly accepted that Bud was not coming back. Bud was gone.

I was heartbroken.

No one could have foreseen the future, but this was what I had feared. I struggled with guilt, fear, the sense of loss, and a feeling of failure. Bud and I had come far, built a friendship, and learned to trust and love one another. My role as rescuer was to restore his ability to trust and to be loved, and I'd been the one to lead him out of his comfort zone into this strange new place.

I could only hope for the best and pray he was safe and content. *Maybe someone had found him and taken him in? Maybe he was trying to get back to the neighborhood he knew?* I'd heard of cats that would travel hundreds of miles to find their home when separated from it. I tried to resist the thoughts that something had happened to him. I prayed every day for his safe return, or at least to know that God had him and he was well.

Several weeks after Bud's disappearance, my mother arrived for a visit. We gathered her things from the car, making conversation when she shared, "There is a cat in the front window of that house just up the street on the left that looks just like Bud."

"Are you sure, Mom?" I asked. "I've looked everywhere for him." *Could he really be just up the road?*

She assured me it was a large, gray tabby and looked an awful lot like Bud.

My heart raced a little as we headed up the street to see the cat that was 'potentially' Bud. I reasoned with myself that it could be, this could be the answer to my prayers! I cautioned myself not to be too excited until I could see this Bud look-alike.

There was no cat in the front window when we arrived, so we left unknowing. But I continued to keep an eye out for appearances. The following week, my husband commented he had seen a similar cat in the exact location, sitting in the house's front window looking out.

Once again, when I walked up the road to see him, the cat was no longer there.

I considered knocking on the neighbor's door to inquire about the cat.

Should I learn the story behind it and see for myself if this could be my Bud?

I was unable to reach anyone by visiting, and there were no cars visible during the day. There was also no tabby to be spotted in the window. On every occasion I passed the house, I would glance at the neighbor's front window. There was no sign of a large gray tabby in the window, and eventually, I stopped expecting to see him.

One day, on my way home, I glanced over out of habit, and there he was! A beautiful, large, gray tabby with green eyes. My heart skipped a beat. Then my mind reasoned out all the possibilities.

This could be anyone's tabby. They were a common cat breed, weren't they?

At that moment, the cat in the window turned his head in my direction and looked me in the eye. There could be no doubt. I saw a flash of recognition. This was Bud!

When the sunlight glinted off his left front tooth, and I saw his oddly shaped front teeth poking out, it was inevitable. My heart lurched, and I resisted the urge to run up to the house and gain access so I could pull him from his perch into a huge bear hug. It was so good to know this was him, and that he was alive and well!

Bud turned his head in pursuit of another interest; I mulled over the situation.

He'd been gone a few months now, and it appeared he was comfortable, content, and enjoying life in his sunny front window, as only a cat can. This was the ideal life for Bud, the life of an only cat, an indoor cat, and it was one I could not offer him inside our multiple cat household.

The flood of feelings consumed me in a rush. In a confusing myriad of emotions, I felt a mix of relief, gratefulness to see him again, and joy at knowing he was happy and living the ideal life. There was also personal loss and sadness. The longing to reconnect and hold him again was so intense it was almost overwhelming. This was Bud, my Bud! Had he been here the whole time, and I'd failed to find him?

As the rush in my heart subsided, I stood just watching him while he lounged undisturbed in the window. I witnessed Bud's utter contentment as he stretched out in the warm window, lazily batting at something in the air, and snuggling in for a nap.

The answer was right there in front of me. Bud was happy, adjusted, and loving life as a cat. He had found a life I could not offer him. I wouldn't disturb what he had found. God was sharing this with me as an answer to my prayers. It was beautiful to see him so serene and content, and provided an end to my fears. While Bud would always have a special place in my heart, I could love him unselfishly enough to let him go. And so I did.

I didn't know it then, as Bud was a friend I made while still new to rescue, but what I learned from Bud was a valuable lesson that has repeated and continues to this day as a part of rescue; sometimes, the job of the rescuer is just a page among the many other chapters of the story. When God calls on us, sometimes it is more temporary than we expect, but that in no way makes it any less important or needed. Bud changed how I viewed my role as a servant in this much needed ministry.

God taught me to be a better rescuer by overcoming the limiting belief that if God sends me a cat, I am being called to be there 100%, from beginning to end, and if I am not, I have failed.

We need to do everything 100%, right? Wrong.

We need to follow his guidance. Sometimes God says, "Nope, you are done. Let go and let them be happy."

Sometimes in our service to others born out of our faith, we plant seeds without knowing how they will grow, BUT trusting that God is at work on His timeline.

My role was not to care for Bud forever, but to help him learn to trust again so he could go on to his intended home. God granted me the gift of knowing I had succeeded in this.

It's been some number of years now since I've seen Bud, but I will never forget him as a friend, and laugh at our antics together, enjoying the particular quirks that make him who he is. Now, added to my fond memories of him is the mental picture of a content kitty stretched out in the sun in the front window just up the road.

> In the morning sow your seed, and at evening withhold not your hand, for you do not know which will prosper, this or that, or whether both alike will be good. Ecclesiastes 11:6

> Love is patient and kind; love does not envy or boast; it is not arrogant or rude. It does not insist on its own way; it is not irritable or resentful; it does not rejoice at wrongdoing, but rejoices with the truth. 1 Corinthians 13:4–8a

Basha

My Calling Angel

The things you are passionate about are not random, they are your calling. —Fabienne Fredrickson

"Here we go, up here, Sweety," I said, moving the feather wand toy vigorously with one hand while snapping the picture with the other. "Nice job. What a beauty you are! So photogenic!"

Part of my role as a volunteer with a local county shelter was to take pictures of each adoptable cat for posting to the adoption sites online so potential adopters could see them. Each picture was accompanied by a little blurb

I created to enhance their best qualities and quirks to capture the attention of the right potential adopter. (That was the simple part, as they were all awesome.) It wasn't always quite as easy to snap that perfect photo!

"Meet kitten, a lively and good-natured kitten. She adores everyone and everything! Her temperament is playful and sweet. She can't resist a good wand toy and loves to purr. She is a snuggler and will make the purrfect pet for the lucky home who adopts her!"

Early weekend mornings were my favorite time in the cat room before the public would arrive for adoption hours. This was the quiet time of the day, where the cats and I could get to know one another. Our mornings consisted of greetings and playtime, distribution of some new toys, or treats, new soft blankets and of course, attention. The honor of assigning their names to go along with their pictures and postings was mine, and I put considerable thought into it based on their temperaments.

Inevitably, one would reach through the bars of their cage and grab my arm or maybe curl up in the corner and cast a look with their beautiful, huge eyes at me. Sometimes their sassy prance around the cage or a voracious attack on a toy mouse would draw me in for a little one-on-one attention.

I was glad to give it, cats in a county shelter have all the odds stacked against them, and any day that did not end in an adoption meant another day in the adoption room. And any day they were left in the room could prove to be their last.

On each visit, I would speak to them in a calm, happy tone to provide a positive energy and let the routine of the morning relax them. I would always pray over them, asking God to let this be the day their adoption happened and given a chance at a new, better life than what had brought them here.

One particular Saturday morning, the cats were settled and calm just before the doors were scheduled to open to the public. The population of adoptable cats was overflowing once again in the room, from the youngest of kittens to adults and the elderly. Weekends were the busiest times at the shelter, with potential adopters streaming through the doorways from opening to close on a good day. More than the normal numbers of volunteers and shelter staff were here as well, working to tidy up in preparation for the day.

It was this Saturday morning that a beautiful 12-week-old Torti (tortoise shell) kitten caught my attention. She had a remarkable, brightly colored coat. Her colors blended together in a mix of fall shades made up of bright oranges and deep browns, with some lighter touches of sand color patches thrown in here and there to add a splash of lighter tones. Just under each of her eyes were a couple of cream highlights sweeping up just to the corners of her dark, beautiful eyes. Her eyes were marked by dark kohl-colored linings that resembled eyeliner Cleopatra would envy. The whole effect gave her an exotic beauty she was fully unaware of. The carefree abandon with which she played radiated an infectious happiness.

She was a lone kitten in her cage (usually kittens are grouped together) playing with a toy dangling in the cage. She was joyful and curious and had been placed in the side corner cage with good visibility to those who walked into the lobby. Something about this little girl's energy and spirit reached out to me. Surely, she would be adopted by the end of the day. I smiled. She looked like a 'Basha' to me, a name that conjured up thoughts of a European beauty, maybe slightly dangerous.

"It's been so wonderful meeting you, Basha," I told her. "I wish you the very best of home to grow up in and belong to. You are delightful." *Yes, she would be adopted before the day was over.*

When the doors opened to the public, a steady stream of strangers would file past the cat room on their way through the front door. The onset of movement and noise was very disruptive, adding to the stressful conditions the cats were already experiencing from the crowded room.

One of the most brutal ironies for cats finding themselves in a county shelter is that the very environment they are forced into defies their most basic instincts and natural behaviors. Everything is sterilized, from the metal cages, to the blankets they sleep on, and the toys that are washed and recycled daily. Cats rely heavily on their sense of smell, identifying, marking, and claiming their personal territory through this sense. The design of the room is cramped, allowing just enough room to stack the cages (2 feet by 3 feet and at least 18 inches high) in a grid, resulting in a forced and unnatural proximity on all sides to other, unfamiliar cats. This is a major source of stress for cats due to their territorial natures.

They are attuned to the mix of intermingled energies all around them; other animals' energy, whether sad or scared, the final energy of souls departing from the euthanasia room, and the excited energy of potential adopters. Shelters contain a potent mix of odors recycled throughout the shelter due to the closed air systems, from cleaning agents to medications, to dirty litter boxes and the scent of multiple other animals causing the distress and fear to mount. Distressed cats often react out of fear by retreating and hiding at the back of the cages, by hissing and scratching, or even biting anyone coming too close. Any movement directed toward them is naturally interpreted as a predatory advance and warrants a defensive reaction. When these actions are labeled aggressive or wild, the cats are considered unadoptable and their fate is sealed.

The biggest health risk to all cats within the room is the recycled air, which circulates through the room and the entire shelter, making communicable diseases more easily transmissible to the entire population. A cat exposed to an upper respiratory infection can spread it to the entire population with one sneeze. This is enough in a county shelter to render the infected cats as unadoptable.

This room holds the most adoptable felines the shelter offers. Only those with the right combination of circumstances, timing, and luck have made it this far and have the chance to be seen and adopted. The amount of time they have also depended heavily on circumstances (appearance, illness, etc.).

Being all too aware of this, as I watched her playing, it occurred to me to put my name on Basha's file to insure she would have someone looking out for her in the event she wasn't adopted right away. It's impossible to know which cats will find their home when. She was really a special soul, and I wanted to see that we gave her a chance at a new home.

This shelter was one of the less affluent county shelters in the area which resulted in low numbers of adoptions and a higher rate of euthanasia. As a result, the shelter had a policy that would allow registered nonprofit 501 (c) (3) rescues to put a hold on cats, so that in the event they weren't adopted by the public after so many days, they would call and then release the pet into the rescues' care. The one stipulation being that the rescue paid the 'pull' fee. As an approved volunteer with the shelter, it afforded me the same option. Many times I had raised the required funds to pull a cat and deliver them into the hands of a reputable rescue. It was not always easy to raise the necessary funds, but by collaborating with the rescues and sponsors, we had a good track record. I stopped at the front desk on my way out and placed my name as backup on her file.

I departed the shelter just prior to the doors opening to avoid the adoption hours. Each weekend, on my return to the shelter, I would make notes of who was no longer in the cat room from the week prior and remove their ads from the website.

One evening, a few days later, I stopped by the shelter on an errand and stepped into the cat room to visit. To my surprise, there sat Basha, playing in her usual fashion. I went to the desk, took the key to the cat room, and entered, eager to greet her and the other cats.

As I was exiting the room, an older lady inquiring about cat adoption approached me. We chatted for a few moments (as cat people do). She asked for my assistance in entering the room to see the kittens.

She walked straight over to Basha's cage and asked to hold her, sharing that she and her husband had seen her the other day on a visit and were taken with her. Her husband was completing the application at the front desk while she visited with her. I opened

Basha's cage (excited and happy for her) and handed her to this lady, observing the care she took in holding Basha. I shared with her the details about Basha we knew, and what a sweet temperament she had. (*How wonderful! She was going home!*)

We were walking toward the checkout desk to finalize the adoption, when a volunteer who had been working the lobby area interceded and loudly commented to the lady that it looked like that kitten had an eye infection. "You oughta pick a different one," she stated carelessly to the lady holding Basha. "That one has an infection."

I was stunned. Double checking her eyes again, I confirmed both were both clear and bright. I asked the volunteer what she was referring to, then I corrected her comment by stating the area she was calling infected was merely the light, cream-colored fur under her eyes. On a dark Torti coat, the white fur around her eye simply highlighted the pink inside lid of her eyes. No swelling, no infection, there was nothing.

As this volunteer shrugged her shoulders and walked off, I assured the lady adopting there was no issue, but offered to have the manager confirm for her. Reassuring her, I worked with the cats all the time, and that conjunctivitis was a common, easily identifiable ailment that this kitten didn't have. (If there had been any infection, most eye infections in kittens are a case of conjunctivitis and are easily cleared up with a little terramycin cream.)

At those words, the lady preparing to adopt stopped and looked at me, speaking:

"No, we don't want a kitten with health issues."

She handed Basha back to me as I tried again.

"There really is no sign of infection," I told her. "It's the white fur under her eyes that makes the red lining of her under eye more noticeable. It's quite normal in a Torti kitten. I promise you, I work with the kittens all the time. There is no infection. We can have the vet confirm and share her medical record with you, if you'd like?"

"No. No. We can't afford to take on vet bills and treatment. I'm sorry," she muttered in reply.

With that, she walked off toward her husband to stop the adoption. I watched as they walked out the door without Basha.

I was aghast at the reality of what had just happened. A thoughtless, flippant comment made in passing by a foolish volunteer had just cost this sweet kitten a home. There was no validity to her comment, but she had driven away an adopter who had been eager to adopt Basha.

I shared what had happened with the Asst. Manager on duty, pointed out that it was a flip comment with no merit, and asked that they address it with the volunteer before she returned to the adoption floor.

Still upset during my drive home that evening, and even now in recalling it, I reasoned Basha was a highly adoptable kitten and the right home would come along. Truthfully, if the couple couldn't afford to care for the health needs of a kitten, they shouldn't be adopting. I turned my attention to planning how to raise the funds to cover her adoption with the shelter if it came to it.

The next Saturday morning, I headed back to the shelter for our routine and to see the cats again. I could access the adoption records (and euthanasia records, which I rarely did) to see what had become of any cats who were not in the adoption room today from last week. I often prayed they had found their home and said a special prayer for any who might not have, and turned my attention to those who were here now in need.

My heart leaped when I looked over and Basha's cage was empty. She must have been adopted between the other evening and now!! I went about working with the other cats with a happy heart.

With the morning visit over and adoption hours to begin again, I headed out, stopping at the front desk to find out more about Basha. *What type of family had adopted her? What day did she go? Perhaps the same lady from the other day had thought about it and returned for her?*

I spoke with the shelter manager on duty at the front desk to inquire.

"Good Morning," I greeted her. "Can you share with me when the Torti kitten Basha was adopted? Was it a family or a couple?"

"What cage?" she asked me.

"She was the 12-week-old here in the side cage, #24?"

The manager entered something into the computer on the desk, then turned back to me.

"No adoption. She was euthanized," she informed me.

My heart fell. The feeling of shock and despair that hit me was a powerful mix, giving way to anger and confusion.

I felt nauseated, but held my composure in place to ask further.

“I don’t understand,” I told her. “Why? What happened?”

She breathed a sigh and returned to look at the computer.

“It says here she was ill, conjunctivitis,” she replied with a noticeable absence of concern.

The surrealness of this conversation faded and the anger rose.

“SHE WAS MARKED FOR RESCUE!” I objected. “Do you see that? It was on the paperwork highlighted in pink. WHY didn’t anyone contact me?” I demanded, trying to keep the indignancy in my voice to a minimum.

“I dunno,” she replied. “Says conjunctivitis - euthanized.”

I pressed on a bit further for more details, but I knew the cause. Basha had been pulled and euthanized the next morning after she came so close to adoption. All due to that ridiculous comment which had no merit, made by a careless volunteer. That volunteer had not only cost Basha her adoption, she had cost her her life. Euthanasia was so commonplace for this shelter that they were numb to the significance of what had happened to this particular kitten.

She was a 12-week-old kitten!? My name was written out clearly on the top of her paperwork indicating I had spoken for her for rescue. No one had called or contacted me, as was the agreement. I would’ve seen that she had any necessary meds or treatment.

The enormity of the cruelty and the blatant injustice shown to this kitten disheartened and enraged me.

I reached out to the rescue network and shared the story with those who were pledging funds to help us raise the pull fee to take Basha into our care. I found my own feelings reflected in their responses.

Behind the restricted signs on the doors leading toward the back of most shelters is 'sick bay,' where the less fortunate felines and other animals are kept. This is the area where the sick, abused, and stressed animals who come in are briefly housed for a variety of reasons, many of which they will not overcome in time to make it to the adoption floor.

Whether the conditions are medical, behavioral, or in some cases tied to a legal issue, no consideration is given to the circumstances of why this occurred. This can be particularly true for cats with a history of injury or abuse, or former pets surrendered to the shelter who are walked directly to the adoption floor with no time to adjust or understand. Shelters do not have the personnel nor the funding to work through the cause or solution for the animals. Once they are deemed unadoptable, euthanasia is the result.

The focus of county shelters, who draw their funding from allotted annual county budgets, is animal containment and disease control, not the welfare of the animals. This is one example of the injustice animals in a shelter system face. The best solution county shelters have designed and implemented on the whole is counterintuitive at best and detrimental to the unfortunate felines who find themselves there at worst.

Their fates may depend on a turn of circumstances over which they have no control. They are given no voice to tell their story and no advocates to speak on their behalf.

There is no one to look out for the welfare and treatment of the pets within that system. It's an injustice in the system and many cats pay for it with their lives.

For Basha, it was as simple as a thoughtless comment, said in haste, that changed the course of her life. This was a circumstance she could not control. Even my attempt to set her up on release to rescue had failed, because Basha had been unreasonably labeled 'sick' and euthanized as a result.

Through this experience and loss, God had awakened in me a deeper understanding of the love and compassion He placed on my heart for His animals. Basha and her experience brought into focus the will to protect them and to cherish them as He does.

Basha had come as a messenger angel to share with me the reality of the conditions of animals in the world and the need to advocate and protect them. God opened my eyes to my true calling in life. The love He had placed in my heart for His animals was a passion. My determination to keep up the vigilance and advocacy for His animals has never wavered. I pray for God to send to me those I can help through His blessings and guidance.

Basha's life story set the stage for my preliminary steps into the world of organized animal advocacy and rescue. She prompted the establishment of "Basha's Fund," an organization focused on raising the necessary funds to pay the pull fees for cats in need. Basha's Fund was dedicated to raising the funds to cover several pull fees in advance. The fund would serve to ensure the required funds were available to assist with these types of emergencies going forward, never again wasting time waiting for donations.

Our local rescue community gained and supported this organized, united program to help save more lives.

A beautiful bouquet of silk flowers was donated from the rescue community to honor Basha and serve as a memorial, and testimony, to the wonderful 12-week-old Torti kitten and her story. This was placed by the front doors of the shelter, with a card that served as a reminder for the inspiration behind Basha's Fund and the circumstances of one kitten's plight.

Basha's Fund became a federally registered, full service nonprofit cat rescue' Doodlebug Manor 501 (c) (3) and continues to be a voice in animal advocacy and rescue following God's guidance and blessings over our efforts.

The general community can be a great asset to local county shelters by opting to offer in -kind donations rather than money. When goods such as beds, food, treats, leashes, etc. are received, the pets gain the advantage of having them to use while they are shelter-bound. Shelters receiving monetary donations must report these to the county as income, which can result in reduced budgets for the next season.

In recent years across the United States, we have seen improvements in the treatment of animals among county shelters with the introduction of nationwide programs like the "Clear the Shelters" campaign promoting adoption of pets at discounted adoption fees.

Foster adoption programs have proven quite successful in placing pets, along with an increase in programs focusing on behavioral needs, training, and a color coding process that helps match the right pets to the right families. Prison Pet Partnerships are proving to be very beneficial, and emergence of nonprofits created to partner with individual shelters is proving very successful in the areas of fundraising and pet placements. These nonprofit groups are governed with a different focus, and their charters allow them to perform many functions that fall outside the county guidelines and bylaws.

The most widespread initiative to spay and neuter all animals that includes funding and low cost programs is imperative to ending the overpopulation so that one day all of God's animals may have homes and the lives He designed them to lead.

The current emergence of Cat Cafes (internet cafes) across the United States is an imaginative and fun approach to adoption that is really making a difference in the lives of homeless cats.

Most cat advocates and rescues look forward to the day we go out of business, because the need just isn't there any longer.

Until then, it's encouraging to see communities becoming more aware and taking an active role in respecting and caring for God's creatures. It's wonderful to see what we can accomplish collectively when others answer the calling God places in their hearts as well.

Who knew that a chance meeting with a 12-week-old Tortoiseshell kitten in a rural Tennessee county shelter would put me on the path of my calling? The events that unfolded around one 3-month-old kitten ignited my passion for animals and their welfare with a new determination and focus. The love God had placed in my heart awakened in a whole new way became my lifelong pursuit.

Basha was my messenger angel and while it was a painful experience, I am grateful for her bringing me God's direction for my life.

> The wise lay up knowledge, but the mouth of a fool brings ruin near. Prov. 10:14
>
> You open your hand, you satisfy the desire of every living thing. Psalm 145:16
>
> And God blessed them. And God said to them, 'Be fruitful and multiply and fill the earth and subdue it, and have dominion over the fish of the sea and over the birds of the heavens and over every living thing that moves on the earth. Gen. 1:28

Cagney & Lacey

Happily Ever After

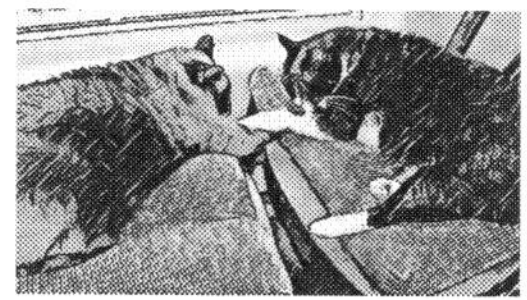

May the road rise to meet you, May the wind be always at your back
May the sun shine warm upon your face, The rains fall soft upon your fields
And until we meet again, May God hold you in the palm of his hand
—Irish Blessing

The unusual request came one afternoon across my work email (via my full-time corporate job outside the rescue). It was a private question forwarded onto just me following a long work-related email trail.

"Is this Lara, Lara from Doodlebug Manor cat rescue?"

A little taken aback, but intrigued, I glanced at the 'from' line to see who the inquiry was from. (Like when you run into someone out of context or years after your acquaintance and scramble to connect the dots. I know I know her...). The name looked familiar, but I could not place our relationship. I greeted her, confirming I was indeed that Lara and waited for the light to shine on how we knew each other.

"This is Cathy," she shared. "Some years ago, you helped me place my adult cats, Cagney & Lacey." Her telling of the circumstances prompted me to remember.

Instantly, the image of these two beautiful elderly cats came to mind. Of course, I remember their story! It tickled me to hear from her, and we began a wonderful reconnection that afternoon.

My first endeavors in rescue had begun by finding homes for and placing cats confined within the cages of the high kill county shelters. Over and over, I was told not to waste my time on the older cats as they were too difficult to place. In fact, the first cat I placed from such a shelter was a 16-year-old black and white male cat named Murphy! (So much for common myths.)

When our rescue gained official federal nonprofit status, as Doodlebug Manor 501 (c) (3), one of the first requests we received was to assist not one, but two 10-year-old elderly cats needing a new home. Two tightly bonded sisters, Cagney & Lacey, had been together in the same house their entire lives. They were inseparable and in need of a new home together ASAP due to a change of life circumstances for their current people. (The first pictures I'd seen of them snuggled together on a chair clearly demonstrated the bond they shared.)

Their owner, Cathy, had done her best to place them with a family, friend, or neighbor, but with no luck. She inquired about surrendering them to the local shelter but was declined and told their chances of adoption were slim at best. After reaching out to a few of the larger rescues resulting in no offers of help, she contacted us to plead their case in hopes of finding assistance.

Both cats were lovely and in good health. Both were medium to long-haired, one (Cagney) was a beautiful black and white girl with fancy white accented markings, silky fur, and a broad rounder face. Her sister (Lacey) was a white-based calico with gorgeous deep tone colors throughout her fur, and a slightly longer face with exquisitely long whiskers. Both were beautiful cats and together they made a stunningly matched set. Their temperaments were even affectionate, and they were the perfect companions to one another. They would be the same for the suitable adopter who would care for them and give them a home.

The exact age at which a feline is considered geriatric in the cat world is subjective. The standard is generally in line with the scale established by pet food companies who define geriatric beginning at age 8 based on nutritional requirement changes that occur.

The number of older cats who find themselves in need after losing a home is sizable and those who wind up in cages at the county and public shelters have an appallingly short window for adoption. Many shelters automatically assign a shorter period for these cats to be eligible for adoption if they allow them on the adoption floor. (For some, it's an automatic sentence of euthanasia.) The cat's circumstances on arrival play a large part in determining their future. Their health, behavior, known ailments, age, and even physical appearance can affect their 'adoption potential' and is at the shelter's discretion. Shelters believe the likelihood of geriatric cats being adopted is much lower than younger cats, or kittens competing for the same homes. There is also the cost factor for the shelter: feeding, maintenance, and the sad truth is that their budget rarely covers medications or treatment for chronic illnesses.

Rescues face the same challenges, and many have a policy not to accept cats over the age of 8 or 10 into their programs believing that no one wants to pay an adoption fee for an older cat who might have a shorter span of years to live when they could adopt a younger cat or kitten. Rescues are also mindful of the costs of maintaining an older cat since it can take longer to adopt them.

Recognizing the need to assist geriatric cats, and the limited options available to them, our rescue works a 'foster' based program to rehome elderly cats. Where possible, the current owner agrees to continue to care for the cats on a 'foster' basis within their home. (Where the cats are comfortable, reducing the stress of one move to foster and then again to a permanent home.) We apply our adoption process from contact, to screening, to adoption to find their forever home. This method has proven to be very effective. For older cats, the foster program, or home to home transition, works most successfully with a smoother transition for all involved, the cats and the humans.

It proved to be a blessing for Cagney & Lacey that the shelters wouldn't accept them. We were aware that it can take longer to find the right fit for older cats and were prepared to work with them. As a smaller rescue, we balance the commitments to cats we can accept to help to ensure they receive the care they need. We could dedicate the time and attention to helping them.

Our rescue works by and through the grace of God. We are honored to work to help our animal brothers and sisters, which God sends our way. Seeking His guidance and blessing over each animal we commit to help is our process.

Cathy agreed to keep Cagney & Lacey in their current environment, allowing Doodlebug Manor to focus on finding good potential adopters for them via our rescue process.

We completed collecting the necessary documentation for the cats that new adopters would want: health records, veterinarian information, details about each cat's personality including any quirks and charming idiosyncrasies. Immediately, we began posting their photos and telling their story through several online adoption and social media sites. Emphasizing their special bond, and relatable stories about them to touch the heart of the right adopter.

The most challenging obstacle facing us was the timeframe they needed to be rehomed. It was mid-spring and the height of kitten season. Most people looking to adopt wanted kittens and they are plentiful this time of year.

We firmly believe the right home is out there for every cat. There is a beautiful match between older cats and homes looking for a quieter, calmer pet. We just needed to find it.

We asked God to watch over these elderly souls and provide for them to bring just the right special home for them. Having to make this transition at this time in their lives was a hardship and frightening, but God would prepare the way for these sweet sisters.

The responses were slow at first, few applications came in the first week or so. Keeping up the mission, we updated their information and changed it up to keep things new and fresh. A few weeks later, we received applications interested in the girls!

Reviewing and screening the applications that came in through Doodlebug Manor, we offered a prayer of thanks when there were a couple that looked like great candidates. We waited anxiously to hear back when we forwarded the two best-looking candidates to Cathy for her review.

As the current guardian for the girls, who would know them better than Cathy? She would be best suited to know what type of home they would do best in and decide who would be adopting. She set up a time for the potential adopter to meet the cats in their home environment (always a perk as the cats tend to be more relaxed and behave naturally within their comfort zone.)

Cagney & Lacey met with their new potential adopter while we anxiously waited to hear from Cathy about how it had all gone. Cathy contacted us, and the news was happy. She was pleased with the lady who had met the cats and felt confident she was offering them a safe, loving home. The adoption was on!

We prepared the final adoption paperwork for the girls and sent it on to the name Cathy provided. The remaining arrangements were worked out, and we set the date for the girls to begin their new adventures in their new home.

A real challenge for older cats facing rehoming is introducing them into a new environment, with new housemates (human, and all others.) These cats have often known one home and family their entire lives. Whether they are experiencing a grieving process for their loss of their home and contentment, or the loss of their owners whom they love, they now find themselves uprooted and facing a brand new environment. (With their territorial nature, this is a considerable challenge for them.) To say this is traumatic would be an understatement. The sudden change and the need to understand how they now fit into this new world can be overwhelming at first. Depending on their circumstances, there is the case of some cats who cannot recover from the loss. (Pets can mourn themselves to death over losing a loved one.) If the new environment also contains additional pets, they must figure out their place in the hierarchy of this new world. It can certainly be a success, but it's just something to be aware of.

The new adoptive home may face the challenge of changes in the cat's behavior due to stress and fear during their adjustment period. It's essential to find an adopter who understands the importance of giving them time to adjust properly and feel at ease. (Who wants to adopt the cat who hisses or lashes out?) Rehoming can be an incredible success with the right environment and the right amount of time and patience shown to them.

The date arrived for Cagney & Lacey to begin their new adventure in their new home. There were tears of joy, relief, and sadness mixed with the excitement over the girls having found a safe, loving place to belong for all of us. The knowledge that these two bonded sisters would stay together for life was priceless. Cagney & Lacey had beat the odds. These two older cats were now home together for good. It is gratifying to help the more senior pets in need.

It's always an unexpected and wonderful thing to realize how much you can come to know and care for the souls that come into your life without ever having met them. We had never met the girls, only knew them through the pictures and the stories Cathy shared with us. We have experienced this several times over the years, but the love, care, and prayer that go into loving them is a bond unto itself.

A new perspective around geriatric cats has been increasing over the last decade where . adopters and rescuers recognize older cats' special attributes and traits. Many specialized programs have emerged within shelters and rescues that focus on matching elderly cats with older people to meet the needs of both. Older cats make remarkable companions for many. So many of these pets have seen the harder side of life and are grateful for a second chance to belong and be loved. (Geriatric cats sometimes fall victim to the system when an owner passes away or is moved into a care facility themselves.)

The importance of planning for your pets, to consider their circumstances if owners can no longer care for them, is crucial to prevent them from ending up in shelters or worse. (Many calls come into rescue requesting we take in cats from retirement homes, long-term care facilities, hospitals, and realtors for those who have not prepared for their pets, leaving them at risk.)

Nowadays, there is an increase in the number of retirement facilities allowing residents to bring their beloved pets. Some have cats that live on premises among the residents and are cared for by the staff. Some programs are set up to allow for scheduled pets' visits to facilities for the benefit of the residents.

The emergence of pet sanctuaries and pet retirement homes around the country provides helpful options for older cats throughout their lives. While some offer the cats a safe, comfortable place to live after the passing of their owners, or for owners no longer able to care for their pets, others offer the additional option for the cats to be adopted again if the right person comes along.

Pet hospices are available for those pets with terminal illness who need caretakers and illness management. Some veterinarians have expanded options for palliative care through end of life, and some facilities are nonprofit dedicated hospice groups.

There are different programs available, and they offer different lifestyle options. As with any pet care program, we strongly recommend reviewing the opportunities and validating their quality of care to ensure they meet your expectations. See the end of the book for more information on additional resources.

Epilogue:

During my re-acquaintance with Cathy, she shared the rest of the story of Cagney and Lacey with me. (A treat we rarely get in rescue.)

Cathy and the lady who adopted the girls had stayed in touch and become friends over the years. They often spoke together about the girls, sharing stories and swapping pictures.

Cathy shared some of these with me, and I so enjoyed hearing about the rest of their story. One picture conveyed much more than words ever could, the bond and commitment of love between these two sisters: both girls laying side by side in their window seats, gazing out at the world in front of them, and holding paws across the space between them! It is a beautiful and powerful picture and how I think of them to this day.

Cagney & Lacey had both lived to ripe old ages. Cagney had lived to be 16, Lacey to 19. They were gone now, but each had lived out their life together, where they were a beloved part of the family.

In ending our conversation, Cathy summarized with this: "Their new home loved them as well as anyone could have. They are wonderful people. They (the cats) did indeed live out their happily ever after."

God had indeed provided all we'd asked for and more, beyond what we could imagine. Proof once again for us as Christians and rescuers, that listening to God and surrendering to His way yields more than we alone could ever do.

Following God's laws might mean that sometimes you break the 'laws of man.' There will be many times in the field of rescue that others will want you to make decisions based on what they have experienced or consider the 'right' way. Many times, they are influenced by a lack of time, finances, or resources instead of making the soul and overall health of the animal the top priority.

Cagney and Lacey empowered me in my Christian walk to rock the boat sometimes, to adapt the accepted standard in order to best serve the animals. While this can be uncomfortable for Christians to do, Gregg and I see time and time again that God will never call you to redefine the 'rules and routes of man' without guiding you as the ultimate roadmap.

> Now to him who is able to do far more abundantly than all that we ask or think, according to the power at work within us, Ephesians 3:20
>
> Do not be conformed to this world, but be transformed by the renewal of your mind, that by testing you may discern what is the will of God, what is good and acceptable and perfect. Romans 12:2
>
> But be doers of the word, and not hearers only, deceiving yourselves. James 1:22

Rascal

Enduring Love

There are two means of refuge from the miseries of life: music and cats. —Albert Schweitzer

Our garage resembled the final blue-ribbon round of a national cat show. If the judges had been looking for these three things, we had it all: Breed, Beauty, and Best in Show. There was the long-haired adult male Maine Coon with his fluffy tail, and a Siamese look-alike female in shades of cream and smokey brown. Three adorable calico kitten sisters with deep tones of fall colors throughout their coats. There were assorted tabby kittens, differing shades of gray and orange, all with the beautiful stripes throughout their fur and the cute white boots on their feet, and one beautiful black adult female, with huge almond-shaped green eyes.

Then there was the small family in the second dog crate from the front.

This mama cat with her tiny offspring were the 'plain janes' of the brood. Mama was a mix of gray, muted tabby and something else, displaying 'out of place' white accents on her coat, and a blatant white nose amid her otherwise gray face. The babies were tiny, barely visible, tucked under their mama's warm belly fur, but we could make out one black/white tuxedo, one gray tabby, and one van tabby, white with large black blotches on her coat. Looking over them all, I giggled and remarked casually to Gregg, "I guess we're stuck with Ugo."

The cats arrived in the early afternoon on a last-minute transport from a high kill county shelter North of Atlanta. This was a mass exodus to save the lives of as many cats and kittens as possible before the massive euthanasia scheduled for the following day.

These cats were coming from an overcrowded and underfunded county shelter at the height of kitten season. It's all too common in rural counties that when space runs out, the cats and kittens run out of time. The shelter had sent out their plea to all registered non-profit rescues and fellow shelters throughout the Southeast region of the US to take in even a few to save their lives. (Knowing it was kitten season and most groups and facilities were full.) We had coordinated with some of our local rescue partners to intake as many of these souls as we could and arranged transport to our location, intending to deliver them to their awaiting shelters over the weekend.

The night before this caravan of hope left, the shelter director had called to ask if it would be okay for them to add in some extra kittens with the nursing mama cats to get them out and to safety. Of course, we'd agreed, and so we really had no idea what our assortment of arriving visitors would be.

In most shelters, the sad truth is the most vulnerable cats and kittens are the first ones slated for euthanasia day when there is no help for them. Those that are injured, have infections, or are older are among the first adults to go. Unfortunately, this can include mother cats and their young kittens (generally under 2 lbs.) who are still nursing or sickly. Small kittens brought in on their own are high on the list as well. Shelters do not have the budgets or staff to care for these tiny ones, and they are highly susceptible to contaminants, often coming down sick.

We settled them all comfortably in the holding area we'd set up in the garage temporarily. (These were our days in rescue before the Manor building existed.) We set row after row of large dog crates up, complete with soft blankets, food, water, litter boxes, and sheets over the top and sides to provide a little privacy between cages. In all, there were 20 or so cats and kittens who had made the long journey and tomorrow their new lives would begin.

My heart was so grateful God had provided the means for these sweet souls to escape and have their chance at a better life. It was a major blessing to see them arrive and to be a part of it. I rejoiced for the cats and kittens on the other similar transports as well.

At the same time, my heart grieved for those not spoken for who hadn't received their 'out' from the shelter, or those who had become sick while staying there whose chance to go was lost. I offered a prayer for their sweet souls to depart this earth and right into the hands of Jesus, I asked that their hearts never know any pain or fear at their moment of departure. Then I offered a prayer that perhaps God might send them back again for a chance to complete the lives they had started before they were taken away.

We settled everyone in, grooming, resting, or nursing their young as Gregg and I took a few moments to walk among the rows of cages, peering over the crew of kitties, and made sure they were secure and happy. Mostly they were exhausted from the long trip, many already asleep. A couple of the older male cats were alert and looking around, while the small group of calicos played together, rolling and pouncing on the new toys they'd discovered in their cage.

Comparing the number of cats that arrived to the number spoken for by the other rescues, I began assigning which cats were going where. Most of the cats were spoken for by the local rescues. That left one group that we would keep and care for at Doodlebug Manor.

Typically, I tried to send the most appealing cats, who would be readily adopted, to the shelters with 'Limited Admission' policies but high-volume adoptions. They would have visibility and a greater chance of being adopted quickly. (Limited Admission animal shelters euthanize animals as a means of population control.) We would reserve the more common looking cats for rescues like ourselves, who were considered 'Open Admission,' in case it took longer to find their homes. (Open Admission animal shelters that only put animals to sleep that are extremely sick, suffering, or unable to be rehabilitated enough to be adopted.)

Over the next couple of days, we had delivered all the cats to their respective rescues. I turned my attention to the mama and kittens that remained with us. We had opted to keep "Ugo" and her babies. On closer inspection, this mama cat was petite, not much more than a kitten

herself with beautiful bright green almond-shaped eyes. She had a short, plush looking coat in the tabby-mix markings with the most interesting white splotches along her belly, front paws, and right in the middle of her face, swooping down and covering that completely white nose that had stood out at first glance. She had a dainty, young face accented by lovely long white whiskers.

Tucked in close, barely poking out from underneath their mama, were the back ends of three tiny babies, their tiny tails barely discernible. These little ones weren't very old at all. When they wiggled around, we identified their little eyes still firmly closed, their ears still pressed flat against their heads, their body size so little they resembled furry peanuts more than kittens. We estimated the kittens between six and eight days old. What a journey these little ones had taken to have a chance at life!

Over the next couple of weeks, the kittens grew and developed rapidly. Their individual coat patterns and coloring became clearer. We had a tiny tuxedo with the white 'ascot' on the chest and two white mittens on the front paws (Myla). The second was a gray tabby with more pronounced tiger-like stripes than her Mama and white capped paws (Lilly), and the little van tabby who resembled a photographer's negative of mama (Rascal). The only difference was that the baby was white with large black splotches and mama was gray with white splotches, but it was the same nose pattern!

Their eyes had opened, their ears were up in little peaked triangles, and their tails looked like miniature versions of a real cat tail. We affectionately refer to this as the "stick tail" age. (The normal age for kittens to open their blue eyes and focus is one to two weeks. Their ears unfold, and they crawl, snuggle, and knead. Kittens' eyes and ears are fully open, though their senses are still developing, and they are standing up around three weeks.

Along this 3–4-week age is when the kittens become more vocal as they start being able to walk, play, and explore their surroundings, they also begin purring. Their teeth are developing, and they play. The kittens became more stable when they'd walk, and it was so much fun to watch them interact and play. We'd closed in an area around the garage that created a little 'kitten obstacle course' providing a small area where they could safely run and play. Placing a child's playpen in the area filled with soft toys and blankets provided another safe area for them to play, and for mama cat to get a break. Mama cats are some of the hardest working parents in the animal kingdom for the first few weeks. Their dedication and care to every need of the kittens is never ending and impressive, but every mama needs a little downtime.

At the five-week mark was when things got very interesting. The kittens' genders were clear, all girls! Their personalities and behavior all emerged. Lilly and Myla tended to be toy-orientated kittens and more content to stay near their Mama (Patience). Then there was Rascal. Aptly named, Rascal was the outgoing, adventurous type who seemingly never ran out of either mischief or energy! She was the kitten always poised to escape when we'd open their cage. Sometimes, clinging to the cage door from the inside with her tiny claws so that she swung out wide, still attached to the door when it opened. She was the kitten set on climbing to the top of the two-story feral cage in the corner in a matter of seconds, then tumbling off before I could reach her. (Thank you, God, she wasn't hurt). And perhaps her most daring feat was charging headlong into the outdoor hockey net, effectively tangling herself up in it, caught by the neck and causing pure panic as we scrambled to cut her loose.

Once the kittens had grown to adoptable ages, and were no longer dependent on Mama, we set them up to find their permanent homes. They had all grown into lovely kittens, and even sweet Patience, who we had nick-named Ugo so long ago, was a lovely girl. We expected them all to be adopted quickly, and leading the pack would be Rascal, with her cute markings and feisty persona.

One by one they were adopted: Lilly, then Myla and then Mama Patience. We were at a loss to understand how Rascal had so few suitors. Left on her own, we brought her inside and blended her with our personal cats so she would be part of a clowder while she awaited that perfect home.

Rascal became a confident, happy cat and easily established herself within our cat community. We're not sure when it became official, but she had made her own place and became a treasured family member. The idea of adopting her outside the family never came up again.

She is an old soul, wise beyond her years. She would look me directly in the eye when I spoke to her, her expressions responsive and reflective. There is a volume of knowledge and experience behind her eyes.

Early on, Rascal set her boundaries within the group. While she got along well with the others, there was an expectation of respect she projected pretty well. The other cats respected her boundaries. On the occasions another cat pushed too far, they would be on the receiving end of harsh hissing, and in some instances, a severe slap.

This was true for humans as well. She did not tolerate strangers touching her and would be quite perturbed with those who dared. Over the years she earned the nickname 'Big Al.' (This was all based on attitude, not her physical size.) Her loyalty to her people was a different story. If you were hers, then she was loving and welcomed a neck scratch or would sit beside you for companionship and a purr. (She is an excellent example of a velvet fist, inside an iron glove!) That didn't imply exemption from an occasional fussing or loud meow of protest. Any attempt to medicate her or cut her nails meant battle conditions.

Gregg and I hosted rehearsals for our band at the house weekly, and in the beginning, our musician friends were all subject to the corrections from Rascal. When she eventually accepted them as her own, then a "Hey Big Al" in greeting and even a head pat was expected from each on their way past her to the music room.

Rascal has remained an animated and lively girl for several years, only mellowing recently in her older age. She is twenty-one now; she's slowed down, walks more carefully, and spends most of her days sleeping in a warm bed or at the foot of the couch with the family. Her outdoor adventures are mostly spent under the backyard shade tree on her lounge pillow beside us.

Although her eyesight diminished, leaving her completely blind some months ago, she is still the adventurous spirit she has always been. We still enjoy seeing her when we enter a room to find her asleep in her favorite bed snoring, or when she feels disorientated and MEOWS loudly for someone to come and find her. She always knows when to appear at feeding time and sits awaiting her meals to be served. With one shake of the treat jar, she begins a circling motion, like a tiny ballerina with her claws tapping the tile floor below. I believe she uses this as her specialized 'radar' technique to zero in on the location to attack the treats.

Rascal has proved to be a sustaining force for Gregg and me in our ministry.

I can't help but smile when I see her and think of what a blessing she is to us. Jesus tells us not to put our light under a bushel, which is precisely what Rascal exemplifies: an uncontrollable, wild beam of light that adds joy and love to our daily lives.

Although rescue can be strenuous, heart-breaking work, God shares gifts like Rascal with us to remind us of the importance of how precious his animals are and why we are called to do what we do. Plus, gifts like Rascal make this type of work so worth it!

It's difficult to describe the amount of love, relief, and hope felt with every successful ending to the stories in rescue when every successful story is another life saved. When the problematic times surround us in rescue, or the numbers seem too many to make a difference, I remind myself that every life saved is another twenty years of love that remains in the world.

It warms my heart that we are here for Rascal in her older age to ensure her safety and comfort. I can't imagine the last 20+ years without her!

Complete my joy by being of the same mind, having the same love, being in full accord and of one mind. Philippians 2:2

Brewster & Lawson

Hail Mary Miracle

The only thing necessary for the triumph of evil is for good men to do nothing. —Edmund Burke

Standing in the back room of the vet's office, my hands were placed protectively around Lawson as he waited patiently on the exam table, unaware of what the next few moments would mean. I was all too aware and could barely breathe. My heart was beating wildly, and my chest felt constricted and heavy. Praying for God's grace over us both, and for strength to get through the next few minutes, we both looked up as the vet entered the room carrying that hateful syringe.

"I'm afraid we don't have any takers," he shared. "I contacted our other clients, but no one has room." And there it was. Our last hope for Lawson vanished, as quickly as our time had that afternoon.

Earlier that day, making my way through the double doors toward the back room copier, I'd taken an 'off limits' detour through the Sick Bay. Volunteers, visitors, rescuers, anyone other than full-time shelter employees were strictly forbidden to be in this room. This area held all the intakes with ailments, injuries, or those on legal hold for the 3-day waiting period after being brought in by animal control.

Lawson sat in the outermost row, midway up the stacked silver cages. He was a beautiful long-haired, mixed breed cat with shades of tan, cream and brown stripes throughout his fur. He had the broad head and meaty paws of a Maine Coon, but a flatter face with a lion's mane surrounding it. His large, bright amber eyes gazed out at me with a soft expression tinged with curiosity.

He was handsome with the attributes most people appreciated in a cat, but his most noticeable feature was the path of painful looking burn marks starting at the top of his head and stretching midway down his back. The fur was singed off, leaving a black trail of semi-closed wounds.

Reading his information card on the front of the cage, I found what I suspected, nothing. No evidence that he had been seen or received any medical treatment. Not even something to ease the pain of the abuse he had suffered at someone's hand *(Just unacceptable).*

Praying over this little soul, I asked God to hold his heart and protect him from any pain he must be feeling. Asking God to please bless us both and grant me the ability to help him, including the strength and wisdom I would need to get past the shelter's front door to find the help he needed.

Without intervention, he would remain in that cage, untreated, until his time ran out. A cat with these types of injuries was beyond the cost, and medical care the shelter could provide.

I checked the time, noting my personal vet's office was open a couple hours longer. They were one of the few offices in town with afternoon hours this late on Saturday, and if I hurried, I could get him there and back before the shelter closed, or anyone noticed he was missing. Assembling a couple of cardboard cat carriers from the back room pile, I began working out my plea to the manager on duty. Talking my way out the front door with permission to take him for treatment was my only hope. (Technically, the cats belonged to the county shelter until adopted, so it would take some convincing to walk out, cat in hand.)

We made a quick stop along the way to gather Brewster, the orange and white tabby I'd promised to help earlier that week, and tucked him into the other cat carrier. He was the next cat on my list to re-home after he had reached outside his cage to tap my arm in a gentle plea for attention. Then he tapped again, as if we were old friends, refusing to let go. In doing so, he had won my heart and my promise to see him into a rescue.

With each cat tucked into a carrier, we prepared to beg permission to take them for treatment at my expense, of course.

"Hey Vanda," I greeted the manager. "I have a couple of the cats we're thinking of taking into rescue, but I want our vet to check them first."

"You can't remove them unless they're adopted," she responded. "They are county property and I'm responsible."

Coming up with the fees to adopt both on the spot was impossible, so I responded quickly.

"I'll have them back, and I'll pick up the shelter's pet supplies and bring them back with me. It's right on the way"? (The shelter had a standing purchase order with a local Co-Op but no one liked to make the trip to get the supplies.)

"Okay, take'em," she responded, "but they better be back here before closing."

A little over two and half hours before the shelter closed. It would be tight, so we left immediately, and I picked up the purchase order on the way.

Our little trio entered the front lobby just as the afternoon office hours began. Lawson purred and rubbed against my legs, weaving in and out the whole time. He explored with a zest and energy I hadn't expected. What a unique, loving spirit he had.

Praying over both cats, I asked God's blessing for them, and for the knowledge and courage to face whatever we would face, asking for a good outcome.

A SNAP test is performed on cats from shelters, or unknown origins to determine their FIV and FeLV status. Awaiting the test results is always tense, as so much of the cat's future can depend on the results. The SNAP Combo Test is used for the detection of feline leukemia virus antibody and feline immunodeficiency virus.) The enigma and fear surrounding the illnesses at that time was high, making the placement of cats with either virus considerably more difficult. For cats inside the shelters, it was a death sentence. Truly, for many cats in general, it was cause to euthanize.

His exam revealed Lawson was positive for FIV, collapsed nasal passage, and severe chemical burns. His prognosis indicated he could heal from the burns and live with one functioning nasal passage, but he'd never get that chance when his FIV diagnosis was revealed to the shelter.

Brewster fared somewhat better; there were no signs of abuse, but his diagnosis was also positive for FIV. No immediate illnesses or challenges to his health, but the FIV+ was unwelcome.

Receiving the news felt like someone had dropped the floor out from under me. It was always difficult to hear this diagnosis, but the odds were stacked against us. This was especially bad news. Technically, they were still the 'property' of the county shelter. (A term that bothers me unendingly that some states still identify living, breathing souls as property.) They would pull both cats from the adoption floor and euthanize them with a positive FIV diagnosis.

I'd promised to return them by the time the shelter closed, but I would seal their fate in doing so. The shelter would leave them both in sick bay to languish until it was time to perform the euthanasia, then it would be a cold, uncompassionate ending. I couldn't do that.

I had promised to help them both, and I meant to do it. The three of us stood there at the crossroad, with no answer in sight. We had nowhere to place them if I took them home, nor did we have the funds to pull them to adopt today.

My mind scrambled to find options, even as the hour approached closing time for the shelter. I could connect with some rescue contacts to see if a rescue who took FIV cats might assist us. Even if the chances were minimal, it was our best shot. There were very few FIV rescuers, and they generally had a waiting list for those cats waiting to get in. I had to try, and maybe we would find an answer.

Dr. Lee, the vet, stood with me for a moment, then inquired what I wanted to do concerning the FIV+ diagnosis.

Overcome with anger and a complete feeling of helplessness, I shared the whole story with him, including our dilemma. I asked him to give me a little time to contact some rescue associates before we made any decisions.

He paused for a moment, then stated, "It's a long shot, but we do have a couple clients who have FIV cats. Let me ask if one of them might be willing to take another."

That was an opportunity for hope! I began reaching out to several fellow rescuers looking for any leads or even temporary care. Burning up the phone lines and my complete list of contacts, each answer came back no. Some people couldn't be reached, some resources didn't work with FIV cats, some were full already, with no room for additional cats. There had been one nibble for Brewster, a possible placement, but it hadn't been confirmed yet.

My last call had resulted in a lead to someone who took in FIV cats, but she couldn't be reached.

By now the shelter was preparing to close, and I couldn't make the deadline to return them this evening. That was one problem, but our immediate emergency was bearing down. I was running out of time on all fronts.

My hope began fading with each 'no' answer. The awful truth was staring me in the face. Lawson's injuries and the FIV diagnosis left him with no options. If I couldn't find a temporary place for him, we would have no choice but to euthanize him. I was determined to do what was best for him, though that decision felt like a knife through my heart.

I cried out in prayer, calling on God in my desperation to provide the way. These poor cats had suffered enough at the hands of humans. (My God, my God, why hast thou forsaken me? Why is thou far from helping me, and from the words of my roaring? Psalm 22)

I looked at this gentle, sweet cat, craving attention despite all he had been through. He'd been let down, abused, and cast away to the county shelter's sick bay, never to be seen again. I felt I had joined the ranks of humans who had let him down. At least I could offer him a graceful ending, administered in a caring environment.

We were at zero hour. I was devastated. I couldn't return these two cats to the shelter for a prison sentence, then death. I stood in the vet's office, praying for God's grace. (God is our refuge and strength, a very present help in trouble. Psalm 46:1)

Coming back into the room, Dr Lee brought the news that none of his other clients had room. No one would take

Lawson. He was standing there with the serum pulled and ready to euthanize when Lawson looked up at me from the table.

The communication was clear. His expression said it all, then his gentle eyes looked at me. I could see he wasn't ready to go. His spirit and zest for life spoke to me through his gaze. He was interested and eager to experience life.

"No," I called out. "I'm sorry, but I can't. I'll find an answer, but this isn't right."

Standing there lost in that moment of uncertainty my cell phone began to ring. I answered to find a return call about the rescuer who specifically took in FIV cats.

"She can take them!" the voice shared. "She'll take them both, Brewster and Lawson!"

She described a wonderful lady (Kat) who specialized in caring for FIV kitties in her home. She wasn't a rescue, but a cat lover with an especially soft spot for the FIV+ cats. A hospice nurse by day, she cared for the special needs FIV cats in her home, providing everything they needed from heating pads and IV fluids to medications and special foods, and especially TLC. She was the blessing we were waiting for! And she had arrived just in time, in a 'Hail Mary' moment!

Arrangements were made, and Brewster & Lawson went home with Kat. We stayed in touch with her over the years (You'll see her again in "Milo") and are so happy to know that both boys finally experienced their happily ever after. Kat was an excellent home for a fantastic pair of cats.

Recognizing the direness of the situation both Brewster and Lawson found themselves in, I immediately heard the voice of God call me to action. The call was so strong and clear that I didn't hesitate to intervene. I wasn't sure how to succeed when I first began this mission, but I know God will take what people mean for harm and use it for good. Additionally, I know God provides us with the means to complete what He calls us to do according to his purpose. It is a requirement to learn these lessons in order to thrive in the field of animal rescue.

In the moments of fear and doubt, when things looked their worst and I could see no way out, I cried out to God in desperation. Putting my complete faith in Him, God answered my prayer with a miracle! (God is our refuge and strength, a very present help in trouble. Psalm 46:1)

This was a pinnacle moment in my Christian life. I truly experienced, for myself, for the first time, the absolute power of Faith. It would not be the last time...

> And he said to the woman, 'Your faith has saved you; go in peace. Luke 7:50
>
> As for you, you meant evil against me, but God meant it for good, to bring it about that many people should be kept alive, as they are today. Genesis 50:20
>
> And God is able to make all grace abound to you, so that having all sufficiency in all things at all times, you may abound in every good work. 2 Corinthians 9:8

Sammy

Let Go and Let God

Cats choose us; we don't own them. —Kristin Cast

There is an interesting phenomenon that occurs with people abandoning or giving up on their pets. They always feel that if their reason is good enough, or if they can convince us it's the only solution they have, they'll be forgiven for doing it. They are seeking permission or forgiveness for the abandonment, a sure sign to me they are carrying much guilt for their decision. And sometimes, when the guilt is too much to bear, they take part in a "dump and dash." (More on this later.)

I have experienced this time and time again for the past 26 years, and I will continue to experience it because there are always pets in need. I pray that someday this heartbreaking truth will no longer be the case, but for now, I have no choice but to rescue. I have no choice but to deal with their guilt-ridden owners. God has put this need to honor and love his animals in my heart. It's the one constant in my life that never ceases, never wanes; it fulfills my purpose. I believe there will never be a last rescue as long as I have breath. Animals and welfare are such an integral part of my heart and soul that they run the gambit of ultra-high and euphoric to devastatingly low and debilitating feelings. The circumstances which bring us together, these beautiful souls and I, vary, and there are as many stories as there are animals. No two situations are the same (which you'll soon read). The one common thread is that God puts me where I need to be to do his will and assist his creatures. That is how rescue works in my world.

That is how my story with Sammy began.

Sammy appeared in the landscaping, under the hedges, just outside the front door of our home late one afternoon, along with his sister Daisy. Two full-grown adult cats, one medium orange tabby male with variations of white across his mostly orange fur, and one tiny female gray tabby with bright white socks on all four feet. They came from out of nowhere, but they came together. That was clear. They had the familiar posture of cats who were comfortable together and stayed close to one another even while exploring their surroundings. There was minimal resemblance in their physical appearance, but that wasn't always an accurate indication of bloodline in cats. (One litter of kittens can have several fathers in their parentage.) They were healthy looking, appeared clean and well fed. No telltale signs of mud or messy, matted fur that outdoor cats usually bore. No collars nor identifying tags, but clearly, they were in unfamiliar territory in our front yard.

I sighed.

These cats were dropped here, abandoned. If not directly in our yard, then at the head of our cul-de-sac, where they'd made their way to the food station we maintained for the feral cats. In truth, that's why we kept the feeding station ready for guests, as a beacon to pull in the wayward kitties who found themselves in need. But it was always heartbreaking to me that someone could just 'dump' a former pet or cat in need with no thought or concern for their future. Just releasing their 'responsibilities' to someone else or for the cats to fend for themselves in an environment they were never taught to survive in.

We never advertised or drew attention to the fact that we ran the rescue here, for the very point of avoiding pets being dumped and abandoned regularly. Word of mouth travels fast and I have no doubt that these two were placed here anonymously by someone who didn't want to approach us for assistance. Perhaps they feared we'd tell them no, or we didn't have room. Maybe they waited until the very last minute before trying to place them somewhere. Either way they were here, and we would help them. (Remember the ole' "Dump and Dash.")

Both Sammy and Daisy were used to people. Working with them and retrieving them was an achievable task. We brought them into the house via cat carriers and got them set up in the extra bedroom I used as our adoption room. (Prior to the building of our first Doodlebug Manor building.)

We would follow the usual steps to get them settled in for checkups with the veterinarian, and to become familiar with their temperaments and quirks. They were both sweet cats, obviously accustomed to indoor living.

Not long after posting their pictures and information on our adoption partner sites the right home came for Daisy, and she was adopted.

Sammy was with us a while longer but seemed content and spent his time gazing out the window tucked into the cat condo or under the bed, cat napping. He'd adapted quickly and had made this room his home. I worried he was grieving the loss of his partner/sister cat, but if he did, he never showed it. Sammy filled out during his first few months with us and was now a large, cuddly boy. He was incredibly strong but gentle (unless administering medications was involved!) and loved the attention of a head scratch or upper back rub.

Sammy was a champ about sharing his room when my mother visited, and the two of them became fast friends. Sammy would even snuggle in to sleep alongside her at bedtime. When she left, he settled back into life in his 'bachelor pad' room.

Four months had passed since we'd welcomed him and it bothered me that no one was interested in making Sammy their own. There is really no way to gauge when the right home will come for each cat. He was such a wonderful, loving cat; I wanted the love and comfort of his own home and family for him. A home where he could be the focus and special pet to someone rather than one of a larger group sharing attention. It didn't seem to bother Sammy; he'd been adapting quite well. I frequently updated his pictures and bio on the adoption sites, but still no response.

His laid-back nature and his choice to remain in the foster room in the house made me feel it was time to start slowly introducing him to our personal cats. He'd been here long enough at this point that he may as well just settle in and not be alone in that room all the time. The run of the house and the perks of being here with us and others of his kind are what I desired for him. I was in no way giving up on a family for him, *but* he could temporarily get comfortable as part of ours.

We began the process by opening his door while supervised, so he could wander out, and our cats could wander in to start the get-acquainted process. Sammy was never too far outside the door frame, with some occasional sniffing of the hallway and staring at the other cats coming to visit. We employed the usual introduction techniques behaviorists teach when introducing cats to a clowder, yet Sammy's choice was to stay put in his room. He seemed fine with what he had and content being a solo operator. (This is not uncommon with adult male cats as some prefer to be 'loners.')

During his first months with us, we had completed the building of the actual 'Manor,' the building where our rescue cats stayed with us while awaiting their adoption. It was a cat house where the cats lived in the same community, with no cages, sharing play areas, food, and even nappy nooks. The Manor provided the opportunities for them to adapt to living in a home while socializing with others (humans and cats). It was completely furnished (cat style with carpets and condos and all manner of toys), insulated, and finished with white paneled walls, and featured a loft area with skylights perfect for cat napping in the sun. Windows overlooked the greenery and garden in the backyard, and with a large window up high in the front, they could sit in to view the entire perimeter of our yard. There were catwalk beams on the inside, and a little front porch leading up to the door. The crown jewel of the Manor was its built-in enclosed 'catio' connected to the side of the building with a cat access door. They could come and go to bask in the sun, catch an evening breeze, or enjoy the catnip garden surrounding it.

We took our time introducing new cats into the group until we knew they were comfortable and content. Cats are amazingly adaptable to their environment when their basic needs are met. This removes the instinct to defend territory or compete for food and shelter. (Cats are one of the few animals who cannot create their environment. They cannot dig or build a den.) Watching them together in this environment really gave us the opportunity to learn so much about cat behavior.

Feeling bothered that Sammy spent so much of his time alone, apart from other cats and cat things, I introduced him to the Manor as well. *Maybe if he could adjust, he could enjoy all the things that were there for the cats. Maybe he'd be just a little less solitary with the opportunity to blend into a group of cats who were accustomed to accepting new members and sharing.*

One afternoon, just before dinner (eating together is one of the behavioral techniques for introducing cats), I carried Sammy out to the Manor, and settled him on a soft blanket on top of the large square ottoman in the front corner. He had this space for himself to observe, settle, and see what he thought of the environment. I stayed with him at first to calm him, reassuring him he was in a safe place. Once he seemed to be settled, I ducked out to let him adjust. Returning to check on him a few times throughout the evening, I noted he'd moved underneath the ottoman, but was still intimidated by the new setting. It might just take a little time (cats are creatures whose contentment depends on routine and familiar territory) so I left to give him that time to adjust and become comfortable. I was so determined to give him the opportunity to explore, and convinced he would begin to like the surroundings and all he could have here, that I left Sammy in the Manor overnight.

I opened the door to the Manor the next morning to Sammy hunched up in the same position I'd seen him the night before. He hadn't moved all night and was still tense. He hadn't calmed or settled in, clearly unhappy in these surroundings. *Had my idea of acclimating Sammy been misguided?* Seeing that he clearly didn't share my desire for him to blend in with the rescue crew, I scooped him up and returned him to his familiar room where he was comfortable. He headed directly to safety under the bed and waited for me to leave.

It was unmistakable: Sammy felt betrayed.

Had I been wrong in assuming he shared the desire to be part of a group of cats? I had envisioned it as a better life for him than the solitary existence he led now.

I was projecting onto Sammy what I wanted for him, thinking I knew what was best for him, without realizing he had already shown me what he desired. Sometimes we are not open to moving differently or in unconventional ways. Sammy wanted to move in a different way than I had imagined. Experiencing the situation I subjected him to ‘for his good’ brought this home.

Similarly, there can be times when we are overly confident in our prayers. We are so sure about what we want God to do that we are not listening with an open heart, but expecting that we know the answers. God knows what the right outcome will be if we will trust him and listen to what he tells us.

If I had been open to considering any other way than my own, and had had a listening heart sooner, I would have saved Sammy from experiencing the pain and fear he felt that night. I could have avoided the guilt I still feel when thinking about that experience I sent him into.

I'm not sure when the shift from ‘rescue foster’ to permanent family member occurred with Sammy, but not having received even one serious inquiry during the time we'd had him, he just naturally merged into our consciousness as family. (Many times, especially during the height of kitten season, the adult cats compete with the younger kittens for adoption. It can take a little longer for the right home to come along for the adults, but it seemed outside the norm that we hadn't had any inquiries for Sammy.) We loved him, and he loved us, and we were all content with that arrangement so that the notion of adopting Sammy faded from our thoughts. He and I had forged a special bond together. He was my boy, and when my mother would visit, well, he was her boy too.

Things went along this way unchecked for a few years. Sammy and the other cats had achieved a peaceful coexistence, but he was not particularly close to any of our other cats. He treasured his solo existence, and so we respected that about Sammy. He was a loner. Perhaps it was his way of claiming territory that was his, a safe spot to belong as a response to having been uprooted and dumped in his past. Abandonment is a cruel, life-changing event for any pet, and some never totally heal from that experience.

One day as I walked through the living room, a lightning-fast blur of orange passed by me on its way up the stairs and into the large bonus room on the second floor. I considered what I'd just seen. *Sammy?* I followed in his wake to make sure everything was ok. Usually, in a house full of cats, if someone is beating a hasty retreat, there is a scuffle, argument, or a standoff happening behind it. I followed Sammy upstairs to find him perched on the rug underneath the piano. No signs of distress, no defensive posture, just a content looking cat.

I was familiar with Sammy's tendency to have personal quirks, but this one took me by surprise. Come to find out, he hadn't just darted up the stairs; he had decided he would live in the bonus room. I had no recollection of having ever seen him upstairs before, but this was where he'd decided he'd stay now.

We maintained most of his regular routines with this slight twist of going upstairs to spend time with Sammy. He was a big love bug, and we spent time together daily. We would stare out the large upstairs window overlooking the cul-de-sac together, or he would join me on the desktop as I worked at the computer. Some evenings, we would curl up together on the couch and watch television. Some days, however, Sammy was shier than others, choosing to stay close by but not directly with me. He was always skittish at the sound of something loud through the window or even footsteps on the stairs. That was his cue to dive under the couch or piano until any perceived danger had passed.

My heart would break just a little for Sammy when this happened. What had triggered this reaction in him? I hated that despite his safe surroundings, he maintained this fear or reactionary response to things around him. I did my best to soothe him each time this happened. He always recovered, but I resented that stress in his life.

Our comfortable routine continued and then one day I learned I required a type of foot surgery with a long recovery rate. This meant using a walker for months during recovery. This also meant difficulty getting outdoors to the Manor building to care for the rescued cats and navigating the stairs that would take me to Sammy.

The frequency of time I could spend with Sammy during this process diminished. I couldn't go up, and Sammy wouldn't come down. My husband saw to his needs, but I missed Sammy and our time spent together, and I know he missed me.

I would call him from the bottom of the stairs and glimpse him now and then in response to my greeting. I would sweet-talk him and try to coax him downstairs for a visit. He never came. At least he knew I was talking to him and trying to interact.

After some failed attempts, I figured out how to 'scoot' up the stairs, butt-first, and avoid putting any weight on my foot. It was awkward, to be sure, but it was beautiful to spend time with Sammy again and love him.

Sammy had aged into an older kitty by this time, so his slowing metabolism and lack of exercise had contributed to some weight gain. It was noticeable even for a big cat; he was plump now, but not obese.

Yet the first day I could make it up the stairs and see him, I immediately knew something had changed. Sammy didn't look well. His fur looked more unkempt these days, and while he would come over to eat, his gait and approach were much slower. Sammy had experienced weight loss to the point he was developing a gaunt look, and his eyes weren't as clear or focused. He looked tired. I would consider these behaviors an onset of the aging process if it weren't for the rapidness of the changes with Sammy. He kept to himself even more now, only coming out occasionally to see me when I'd visit.

I commented on his state to my husband, and he had also noticed the changes in Sammy. We had just lost our other orange tabby (Baxter) to pancreatitis. With Baxter, it had come on suddenly, presenting itself as an Upper Respiratory Infection, and we'd treated him accordingly. When he showed no improvement, we hospitalized him hoping for the best, but were forced to watch him decline until he had passed. The ailment had been unpredictable. (In fact, the vets had expected full recovery for Baxter based on his labs.) Baxter had been the same age Sammy was now

Confronted with similar symptoms in Sammy, including the same rapid decline. We were staring into the face of what we suspected would be an eventual loss; this could also be pancreatitis. We refused to give up this soon, but also determined not to put him through what we'd seen with Baxter. When the time came, we would decide what was suitable for Sammy. We were huge supporters of quality of life over quantity when it came down to it and were determined not to see another pet diminish and suffer based on false hopes of blood panels and testing results. While we were grateful for the medical care and medicines available to our pets, this was not a decision to be left to science. We would follow our hearts and pray. We knew our boy better than anyone else, and through the pain and anguish of making a final decision, we knew God would guide our hearts. He'd done it before, and if we'd heard him sooner and recognized his voice, things might've gone differently for Baxter.

The inevitable loomed large in our hearts, but we watched over Sammy daily and prayed. One morning as we were waking up to prepare for the upcoming workday, Gregg made his way down the hallway to the kitchen. Before I could get up and onto my walker, I heard him call him from the other room. The tone of his voice telling me something was clearly wrong.

"It's Sammy," he called out. "You'd better hurry."

I struggled to move as quickly as I could and get to them.

When I made it to the living room, there at the bottom of the stairs, curled up on a blanket, was Sammy.

Sammy didn't look good at all. I struggled from the walker to the floor and scooped him into my arms. He meowed at me, looking in my direction without really seeing me. His eyes were glazed over with an opaque white film. I buried my face in his side, feeling the soft fur, and trying not to cry. I didn't want him to pick up on my sad energy and fear and react to it. Sammy was diminished and lethargic. My big, cuddly boy seemed so small and frail, and when he looked up at me the second time, I knew.

There was a soul-to-soul connection, and I knew instantly God was sending me the answer for Sammy. Sammy, my boy who never came downstairs, had made it all the way down that staircase in his dilapidated state to see me and say goodbye. Not only had he made it down, but he was waiting for me to come to him. I held him and felt the struggle inside my little man: his body was failing him, but his spirit would not let go. His unbridled loyalty wouldn't surrender.

Now, I allowed the tears to come. We both knew this was goodbye, and it was okay if Sammy knew I would feel this loss of him and how much I would miss him. But still, he would not let go.

I whispered to him, reassuring him it was all ok. It was ok to leave; he would be fine. He didn't have to stay for me. I would miss him, but it was time for him to go home. He'd been a good cat and so loved, but better things were waiting for him in Heaven. Still, he resisted, though I heard his breath become more labored and ragged.

I prayed for God to take him, to not let him languish here in this state. I prayed God would touch his heart and tell him it was okay to let go and be at peace.

"Sammy, let go," I told him. "Run to those waiting for you. Run to your loved ones who've come to lead you home. I'll see you again one day, love."

The moment the words were out, this frail, beautiful boy summoned his remaining strength and ran. Whatever or whomever was waiting for him was so beautiful, he was running to get there. His legs moved as if he were going as fast as he could run. Then, with one tiny meow, he was gone.

I felt his soul leave and experienced a feeling of loss, but also pure joy for him. I knew God had him at that moment. He was safe and whole again.

Gregg and I sat for a moment in stunned silence. Sammy was gone. We reflected on the miracle we'd just witnessed when Gregg broke the silence, stating, "I wouldn't have believed it if I hadn't just seen this with my own eyes."

Even now, when I think of Sammy, I genuinely believe I never found the home I was seeking for him because, in his heart, he knew he was home with us. He knew where he belonged was here with us. I'm so glad he did. What an honor and a blessing to have been given this wonderful soul to look after, and to have him in our lives. Someday, we'll see him again.

> Trust in the LORD with all your heart, and do not lean on your own understanding.
> In all your ways acknowledge Him, and He shall make straight your paths. Proverbs 3:5–6

Lucy

The Overcomer

When I look into the eyes of an animal, I do not see an animal. I see a living being. I see a friend. —A. D. Williams

Lucy's cage looked out over the side parking lot of the county shelter; the view was concrete. If you looked far enough past the parked cars, a tiny slip of grass was barely discernible, blended into the horizon. This is how she spent her days, staring out her window relentlessly toward that tiny patch of nature so far away from where she was now.

She had the misfortune of being a short-haired, black cat, petite and timid with sad eyes, and a weathered-looking fur coat. Nothing about Lucy stood out at first sight in a room full of 30+ cats and kittens, of varying breeds, ages, colors, and sizes. Here they were all competing with one another for a home from among a limited number of potential adopters. That was the way to escape the conditions of this room and to find a much better life.

They confined the cats who found themselves here inside cages stacked in rows along the walls, within close proximity of each other. Each cat is surrounded by other strange cats, and even for those with a hiding place in their space, like a cardboard cat box (crucial to relieving stress in cats), the result would be an even more cramped environment. Typical cages are 24 inches wide by 28 deep by 24 high.)

You can imagine the shock, fear, and uncertainty most cats experience when they are suddenly taken from the life they've known and are thrust into this strange new way of existing that defies their very natures. There is little opportunity for time outside this limited space, if any, and very little that occupies their interests or engages their instincts. This is a harsh reality for any animal, particularly cats, who are territorial by nature. In some cases, there is very little time between when they leave their environment and are forced into a whole new existence. Whether surrendered from the home they've known or picked up by animal control, the next stop is a noisy, unyielding environment, where they are placed into these cat rooms at the shelters.

Rule one in the shelter environment is that everything must be washable, removable, and replaceable. The method eliminates as many contaminants as possible to prevent the spread of anything communicable. The result is a cold, sterile environment, with nothing that remains constant for the cats to 'mark' or rub their scent onto, establishing their territory. Even the comfort of a soft bed or a favorite toy will be removed and replaced by a strange one. This removes any possibility of something familiar and comfortable remaining with them to ease their stress.

The closed system of air filtering used recycles air throughout the room, bringing with it the scent of strange animals, the harsh odor of chemicals and cleaners, and smells from a veterinarian clinic, all mixed with the residual scents left behind from people who had come and gone throughout the day. All of it is unfamiliar, and none of it welcome or comforting.

Kittens, in general, fared better in the shelter environment; being young and small, they often shared a space and entertained one another by playing. Kittens also have a higher rate of adoption, resulting in less time spent here. For the adults, anything different from their daily routines was interesting and irresistible to watch. It might mean fresh food or a bright new toy was coming their way. There was the potential to interact with someone, maybe even play or be taken out of the cage and held. When someone entered the room, the more outgoing kitties would draw attention to themselves with a meow or reach out from behind the bars of their cage to touch an arm, hoping for companionship and maybe some comfort.

In response to these conditions, some cats experience 'shelter shut down' as they try to adjust. Shelter shut down occurs when cats become distressed and display apathy, becoming lethargic. Often refusing to eat or care for themselves, it's as if they've given up. Sometimes they behave defensively out of fear by hissing and even biting when approached. For many cats, once removed from the stress of a shelter environment, they show improvement within days. Sadly, some never do.

All too aware that Lucy's behavior pointed to this; I kept an eye on her. I spent extra time with Lucy to entice her to interact with me. Bringing extra treats to get her to eat, petting her gently, and trying an assortment of toy types had no effect. I chose a clean, soft blanket to put down for her, spreading it in her area, but she barely moved. I spoke to her reassuringly, encouraged her to eat, and tried coaxing her to look at me to pose for a picture or two to post her for adoption. Lucy continued to stare out the window as if I weren't there. Her heart belonged somewhere else, and her will to continue was waning. She was reaching the critical point rapidly.

Notifying the manager on staff of her condition, I put my name on her file to hold her for me if not adopted in the next couple of days. The odds were barely above none that a remote, quiet, small cat in the corner would find her home here, but the public had the first right to adopt, and Valentine's Day weekend was approaching.

That evening, I took Lucy's pictures and wrote up her story. Taking great care to outline her potential and what was happening to her in the shelter environment, I circulated her story via social media with some poignant pictures of her staring out the window. Showcasing her forlorn and desperate circumstances, I wanted to reach out to the rescue community, veterinarians, and any potential adopters trying to secure a better life for Lucy.

We received some donations in response to contribute to her care, but not enough for us to pay her fee, pull her from the shelter, and get her the help she needed. No one was stepping up to offer her a home, the break she so desperately needed. Time was running out, Lucy was losing weight by the day, while I struggled to pull together the funds to pull her and get her some medical attention.

The ride home brought me into a conversation with God. I shared my fear and sorrow about this little lost soul, praying He would protect her, and breathe hope into her heart. I prayed God would fill her with encouragement and let her know someone was fighting for her. Lastly, I prayed God would show me the way, empower me to help her. Little did I know what God was up to...

Days later, a fellow rescue friend and I set about cleaning and decorating the cat room with festive hearts and colorful decorations to prepare for a big holiday promotion. Once decorations were complete, each animal got a cheerful handkerchief-scarf and an extra round of treats. *There's no better holiday to call attention to these animals' needs than the day of love, right?!*

From the time the shelter opened that weekend, until the last visitor had left and the doors closed, the adopters had shown up in droves! Dogs, cats and a wayward chicken were all adopted. It was a successful weekend with many deserving pets adopted. So many cats had found their homes! But not Lucy. My heart sank at the sight of her still sitting there in the same position. One more time, I encouraged Lucy.

"Hang on, little girl," I told her. "We're almost there. It will be so much better soon."

I prayed again there with her in the room, asking God to help me help her.

Reaching into her cage, the large-eyed, painfully thin cat I found there jarred me. Lucy was wasting away to nothing but bones with a dead look in her eyes. There was no more time to waste. I would return in the morning and take her out of here for her much-needed help. I would find the money.

I alerted the manager that I would be by in the morning, first thing, to get her and take her in under our group. They had closed the books for the night and wouldn't process a transaction until the morning. We were not quite a rescue group yet, but a fund that was organized to raise the adoption fees for needy cats. This little girl had no more time to wait. I would find the means to help her.

"Just hang on for me, Lucy, just one more night," I whispered to her. "Please don't give up. Tomorrow is the day your life will change. I'll be here to get you."

That evening, I arranged to get Lucy set up at home and called the veterinarian, explaining my concerns and preparing to take her directly there the next morning.

It was a restless night; I was concerned about her and desperately did not want her to give up over the next few hours. If she would just hang on, I would come to help her just as I'd promised her I would. One last time I asked God to help her hold on, to let her know I was coming, and to ease my stress. God had this.

I arrived before the shelter opened the next day and finalized the arrangements for Lucy. Some additional funding had come in overnight due to a desperate last-minute social media frenzy on her behalf. God had heard her heart and mine. We were just shy of having enough for her fee, so Gregg and I squeezed the grocery budget for that week and donated the rest.

Walking in the front door, I was nervous and excited all at once. I glanced at the window to see little Lucy in her usual position. I stopped at the front desk to get the fee and paperwork finalized, securing her freedom. Making a straight line to her cage, I was excited to see her and tell her this was the moment she'd been holding on for.

As I arrived at her cage, the manager on duty was standing at the cat room door announcing that she was pulling cage 16 for the back room. In that instant, my jaw dropped, and my heart started beating wildly.

Cage 16 was Lucy!

Pulling anyone from the cat adoption room for the 'back room' meant Lucy was being pulled to be euthanized. I hurried to the front of her cage just as the shelter manager was reaching to pull Lucy out of her cage to move her to the dreaded back room, informing her I had just adopted her and was here to take her home. She was coming with me.

She blinked slowly, then looked at me, stating, "This cat is too thin, there's nothing left of her. Choose a different one."

"No," I responded. "This is the cat I came for this morning. Her paperwork is processed, she's adopted."

As I spoke, I moved over in front of Lucy's cage and reached in to claim her. Wasting no time, I placed her on the warm, soft blanket in the cat carrier and secured the door. We headed promptly out the front door and on our way to the vet. God had heard us and provided the way.

Shelters can be unpredictable, although we followed the guidelines to mark her file, and took precautions to tell the manager the evening before of our intentions, they were overlooked, almost costing her life. We had just made it under the deadline this time.

Bending down to reassure her, I spoke, "This is the beginning of a new life for you, Lucy," I declared with renewed hope. "I promised you I wouldn't leave you there on your own. God is looking out for you, little one."

Arriving at the veterinarian's, an exam, IV fluids, supplements, and a beginning prognosis later, Lucy would stay as an inpatient over the next few days. She was dangerously thin (2 pounds for a grown, 2-year-old cat), dehydrated with a host of other issues to overcome to return to health. The biggest of all would be reviving her will to live. Lucy had a chance now, however large the undertaking seemed, we would take it.

This journey for her would be daily, step by step, prayer by prayer. I'd learned early on to never underestimate just how powerful a recovery could be when love and support sustained a patient. God had heard us and provided the way through the struggle. Lucy remained hospitalized over the course of several days, and every day I checked on her prognosis and visited to keep her spirits up. After her initial week, she was making progress and was still in the fight, though she had a way to go. There was improvement! I made a big deal of sharing this with Lucy and accepted that as the first milestone in this fight!

Lucy slowly gained back some strength and was healing. Hope had returned, and she was making progress daily. Meanwhile, I continued working to gather funds to cover her mounting medical costs, and to find a suitable placement for her upon release from the vet. Lucy had survived and was improving daily, but would still require a high level of care to make it back to health.

It had taken much longer than expected to raise the funds needed to get her out of the shelter, and we almost lost Lucy. The reach of available funds and donors was limited, and we needed the ability to respond more quickly when the needs arose. As a result of Lucy's struggles and the need to find solid funding sources, we registered as a 501 (c) (3) nonprofit rescue. This would open the door to grants, funding, and the ability to solicit funds from larger groups and participate in larger initiatives. This was the beginning of Doodlebug Manor 501 (c) (3) as a federally recognized cat rescue.

As Lucy showed signs of recovery, I continued to work ahead to find a wonderful placement for her. Recently, I met a couple at a local rescue gathering who were operating a fairly new 501 (c) (3) sanctuary specializing in hard to place animals and hospice care. We knew several rescuers in common and so it seemed a blessing when they reached out in response to my inquiries around Lucy.

They were situated on a nice homestead with land, already established, and working with a small group of dogs. There was a nice, designated cat area, in addition to having the run of the inside of the house.

We discussed Lucy's special needs and her path to healing. As a registered nurse, the wife of this duo could provide fluids and additional supportive medical care

Lucy would need for a full recovery. Arrangements were made, so Gregg and I drove out to their location to meet, observe the conditions of the sanctuary, and gauge the welfare of the pets already in their care.

The area set up for the cats turned out to be a full upstairs, one large room of the house with ample windows and room to stretch out for fun and play. The room had been tailored to the comfort and needs of the cats with plenty of condos, sleeping areas, and toys. The property was fenced and surrounded by farmland, so the cats were set up with an opportunity to be outside in their environment as well. I intuitively understood this would appeal to Lucy.

The pets on premises all looked healthy, happy, and well adjusted. With this and the recommendations from several of our rescue community, the sanctuary seemed like the ideal location for Lucy to graduate from the vet, and to get the personal care she would still need for total recovery.

This location could provide a healing and homelike environment for Lucy. She could continue to heal, both physically and mentally, in a comfortable environment and still have access to the medical care she would need.

We were overjoyed. This looked like the new beginning for Lucy's future. God had provided above and beyond what we even thought to hope for. Our hearts were light and optimistic.

The first couple of nights following her release from the hospital, Lucy spent with Gregg and I at home. We wanted to assess her progress and keep her comfortable, maintaining her schedule of medications and meals, before taking her to the sanctuary on the weekend.

We shared with Lucy all about how wonderful this new life would be for her. The freedom she had longed for was going to be hers. All she had to do was heal and be happy.

When the morning arrived, we drove to the sanctuary and slowly introduced Lucy to the new environment. We walked the entire area with her, exploring and letting her investigate as she looked over every corner of the house. She took her time inspecting the entire cat area, sniffing and getting oriented. She would have one companion, George, a friendly, large, yellow tabby. They sniffed and greeted one another, seemingly at ease together.

Confident that Lucy would be comfortable and well cared for here, we said a tearful goodbye. After the journey we'd been through together, it was difficult to walk away. Knowing she was in good hands, in a location that offered more for her than we'd hoped for, helped to ease our anxiety. We planned to come back and visit once she settled in.

We received wonderful updates on Lucy's progress, and as she felt at ease and her temperament began to shine, we learned about her unique ticks and quirks. Lucy was doing well and got along wonderfully with George. She didn't mind the dog companions and had grown particularly close to the man, making the back of his easy chair in the living room her favorite spot to sit. She would sit with him in the evenings, gazing out the large window that overlooked the farmland and fields, and her gaze was content. It was such an improvement from the lost, lonely cat that had all but given up inside the shelter.

Lucy loved food from the refrigerator and each evening would wait until she had won the prize of a cold cut or other treat. She looked like a different girl. On our follow-up visit, we noted how solid she was now. She had gained a good amount of weight, and her eyes were alert and clear. Her jet-black fur was glossy, and she looked content, poised on the back of her favorite chair. I snapped pictures of this new, happy Lucy as a reminder of how far she had come. Her story was that of a true champion, a champion that not only survived, but thrived and was open to living a joyful life.

We checked in with George before preparing to leave. Patting his head and wishing both cats the best new lives, Gregg and I left.

The picture I had taken of Lucy that Valentine's Day so long ago, the small listless cat wearing her little kerchief and staring off into the distance, longing for something she had once had, remains on my desk to this day. Lucy provides inspiration on the hard days in rescue and serves as a reminder that even the smallest act of mercy and love to help another can lead to such blessings!

While it captured a heartbreaking moment in time, it serves as inspiration to me to keep fighting the good fight for the real underdog in the animal rescue game, cats. I am always grateful and joyous for the happy endings we get to witness. Though rescue stories do not always end happily, moments like these sustain me.

Lucy was settled, content, and recovered. It was the outcome we had prayed for, and Lucy had worked hard to achieve it. I was so proud of her. This time when I left her at the sanctuary, she was home.

Or so we thought...

> I have said these things to you, that in me you may have peace. In the world you will have tribulation. But take heart; I have overcome the world. John 16:33

Dusty

Our Christmas Guest

"The quality of mercy is not strained;
It droppeth as the gentle rain from heaven
Upon the place beneath. It is twice blest;
It blesseth him that gives and him that takes."
—William Shakespeare

Carols, bright twinkling lights, ribbons, and packages everywhere. Christmas was less than a couple of weeks away. Retailers had pulled out all the stops on their commercial budgets, and there was the delicious scent of seasonal goodies. The local churches were busy preparing for their special services, and families were making plans to celebrate the holidays with family and friends. Well, most families anyway.

Preparing for the Christmas festivities ourselves, we were busy decorating when the call came into the rescue: someone desperately needing to surrender their elderly cat. This was an all-too-common theme, and the state of what constitutes desperate is a subjective term at best. The result is the same. However, some poor elderly cat was about to lose the only home and family he'd ever known just before Christmas. He needed help.

It's a cruel situation for an elderly cat to find himself in, but there he was, and we were his last chance. According to his former family, they had tried unsuccessfully to find him a placement with several rescues and shelters, but none would take him in. We could take him and couldn't bear the thought of him in a shelter or worse, alone at the holidays. With the decision made, the future was set for this cat. He would be our Christmas gift!

We agreed to take him, deciding for his former family to drop him off at our trusted vet's office. This is a practice we started long ago with our vet's cooperation, so that any new cat coming in came with a medical checkup and we knew their status. This was especially important as we were still doing foster and rescue out of our home. The Manor building itself was a couple of years in the future, so we always took extra precautions to limit the exposure or spread of contaminants among our healthy, vetted herd.

This was our introduction to the sweet older cat we called Dusty. He was a beautiful, short-haired, 16-year-old orange tabby. Lanky and tall, he was a handsome older gentleman, with big, beautiful eyes, and alternating dark and light rings of color on his long, long tail. He had meaty paws, despite being a slender fellow. His fur condition looked pretty good for his age, and he was alert and curious. Likely, he was scared and unsure of what was happening, but he was gentle, sweet, and trusting even during our first encounter. It was going to be so easy to love this boy.

We left the vet's office with Dusty in tow and chatted to him all the way home about how he would be happy with us and we would make him feel welcome. He would belong with us until his new, forever home (this time) found him and welcomed him. We'd make sure he never wanted for anything in his older age. I offered a silent prayer of thanks that God had entrusted us with his care and prayed for the wisdom to know just what those things would be for Dusty.

There is always risk involved in bringing an older cat into an existing clowder. They can be introduced into the herd and with a bit of time, adjust to being the new kid. They will find their place with patience and love, but there can be some standoffs and hissing matches until the hierarchy adjusts. (It's never a guarantee.) We had no real idea what his experience of living with other cats looked like, or how he would do in a sizable group like ours. But our group was used to new members making an appearance in their world and we'd never had an issue of non-adjustment yet.

Arriving home with Dusty in the telltale cat carrier, our existing cats knew the routine, someone new was arriving. Dusty had done well at the vet visit and on the car ride home. Now he faced the biggest challenge yet: figuring out what was happening and facing a new group of cats in a strange environment.

Our usual process involves placing the carrier in an area against a 'safe' wall (so their back is protected) and sitting next to it, slowly introducing everyone in calm, relaxing tones. The next step was slowly introducing the cats by putting Dusty in a 'protected' dog cage set up with the necessities and comfort items with separation for his well-being. Removing the stress and anxiety at the first few moments of introduction for all the cats involved was crucial. It would determine how well the adaptation process would go.

Peering out of the cat carrier into the faces that crowded around to greet the new guy, Dusty seemed to embrace the challenge as an opportunity devoid of anxiety and instead full of interest. There was some usual sniffing and greeting behavior, but no animosity on either side of the carrier door. This was a great start. Dusty purred inside the carrier and appeared relaxed, reaching out through the carrier grill (door) with a paw to make friends with Gregg. When we opened the carrier to get Dusty settled, he reached up and put his arms around Gregg's neck in a fiercely gentle but determined hug. This was one sweet cat.

Dusty charmed us all in a matter of moments. He was just that cat. Calm, unassuming, a gentle soul just taking in life and all the new energy of his surroundings. Surprisingly, he blended in quickly, establishing himself as part of the gang. He was a quiet cat and seemed content just to belong.

Christmas was growing closer, and as we talked with friends, (Marci and Rex, you'll see them again...) we shared the situation about Dusty, our latest foster and what a great cat he was. How well he had done coming in and adjusting, and how mellow and easy he was to love. Before the conversation ended, they had opened their hearts and Dusty had found a home to go to. And not just any home. This is the jackpot of dwellings for a cat. Our friends were cat lovers and had other cats at home, so Dusty would have a pack to belong to after leaving ours.

We couldn't wait to share the news with Dusty. His Christmas miracle arrived early, and he was going home. His new family would be there to pick him up just after Christmas when they returned home from holiday travels. Everything seemed to be going right for Dusty.

We were grateful and happy, thanking God for providing the most fantastic home for Dusty. This was a home we were incredibly excited about, as our friends had a lot of experience with all ages of cats, and they had a wonderful, peaceful home.

Dusty's favorite pastime was sleeping on the back of the sofa and snuggling into a cushion. Even in the middle of cat chaos, (a rousing toy chase or a spit fight over who got to the sofa first, you know, cat stuff) he was totally content. That was yet another blessing we were grateful for.

I observed that while he was content to sleep and watch the goings-on around him, not out of character for a cat his age, he ate very little. While the other cats heeded the call of the wild at dinner time, storming like a herd of tiny buffalo to get there, Dusty would saunter over and nibble a little, but that was it. This too could be a condition of aging and inactivity. When it became clear over the next couple days that he was losing weight, alarm bells went off and we went back to the vet. This time, we knew what we were facing with a follow-up exam and a couple of blood panels.

Dusty was in an advanced stage of thyroid disease.

I quickly passed through the typical reactions of unwelcome surprise and grief, setting them aside for later, and focused on discussing treatment options for him. *Medication? Surgery? What are the possible outcomes for an elderly cat with advanced thyroid disease? What were the costs? What did recovery look like? Was recovery even an option? What do we do to keep him eating and as healthy as possible in the meantime? Would his new adoptive home still be able to take him in?*

With a case of thyroid disease as advanced as Dusty's, we were limited in options, but both were surgical remedies. Surgery was a significant risk for a cat of his years, but without it there would be no future. The surgical procedure would offer some limited potential for more time.

This was a painful decision, trying to determine what was best for another living being, what Dusty's wishes were. We didn't have the luxury of direct communication or an ELD (End of Life Directive) to consult, and Dusty wasn't offering any hints.

Asking God for His guidance, to tell us what was meant to be, what was in Dusty's heart? What was right for Dusty? Weighing the options and knowing Dusty had a good quality of life with us, and a wonderful home to go to when this was done, we left with a date set for surgery (December 27th). The surgery removed part of the thyroid gland to buy a little more time for Dusty.

God had entrusted him into our care and if there was any chance for his happiness, we were going to fight for that.

This way, he could live out his remaining time through recovery with us. He would enjoy his new cat friends, be protected, fed, comfortable, and' most importantly, loved. Still fearful of the complications elderly cats can encounter during surgery, including death, we listened even more closely for God's voice to tell us this was the right decision.

Christmas was just a couple days away; we left the vet's office heading back home so he could enjoy the spoils and excitement of the holiday season. Since the future was uncertain, we would enjoy his time with us and we began spoiling him. We would love him through all the changes he had just recently endured and be with him through whatever his future held.

My mind returned to the family who had surrendered Dusty to us "desperately needing" to rehome him just days before. While a myriad of emotions and thoughts flooded my heart, I wondered at the pure cruelty of their actions, and a lesson formed.

Why would anyone surrender their lifelong pet, knowing he suffered a terminal illness, and not disclose it? Why would they put us through falling in love with this boy only to suffer the discovery that he was terminally ill? Worst of all, why would they cast him out of his home, making him adjust to a new reality in the state he was in? WHY hadn't they just told us he was sick, and they couldn't afford the treatment, or didn't they care enough to bother?

Knowing he was facing an illness wouldn't have deterred us from helping him, and at least we wouldn't have wasted time in discovery and sought help for him from the start.

As I worked through the anger and outrage of what these people had done to this beautiful soul, capable of giving unconditional love the way he did, I finally rested on the premise that there was a reason God brought Dusty to us. This precious soul deserved to be where he was loved and cared for during his time of need. Being with those who would look out for him, ensuring the best for him, was our commitment to him.

We reached out to our friends to inform them of Dusty's condition. In less than a beat, they asked us to keep them informed about how he was doing. Of course, they would wait for when he was ready to go home! It was still on; now it was up to Dusty.

Over the next few days, Dusty's health and appearance markedly declined. We watched helplessly as the disease increasingly took over. We prayed and held on, encouraging him to hang in there through Christmas. Help was coming. Time was just not on our side. We reminded him how a new loving home awaited if he would just fight through it a little longer.

And while I know he did his best to hang on, Dusty left us just before Christmas Day. Quietly and unassuming, just like he had arrived. It devastated us. The feeling of having just missed the mark was overwhelming and mixed with our grief and sadness.

After the initial shock, we took solace in knowing that he knew he was loved and that we did what we could to care for him while he was with us.

God had called him home, and so he had gone. We imagine him leaving his worn-out, broken body here on earth and heading straight into God's loving arms. His soul was renewed and carried with it the love he experienced here on earth.

God had spared us the choice of wondering if we were doing the right thing. Dusty was far too sick to have survived the surgery, and while we didn't know that at our point of deciding, God did.

We'll never know what Dusty's life was like before, but we loved his wonderful, bright soul in the short time we knew him. We know Dusty taught us a couple of important lessons.

The first being God's purpose for us in rescue is not always to be there from steps A to Z. Sometimes, our purpose is to step in, temporarily, at the point where we are most needed and provide love and care to those with whom we are entrusted. We are not always called to stay and serve for the long haul for each cat we serve. Our purpose was to love Dusty and send him home to God, knowing that his life and existence mattered. Our part was to ease his burden and worry when he needed it most. He left a memorable mark on our hearts. After all, it can never be wrong to offer love and compassion to those in need. (Be merciful, even as your Father is merciful. Luke 6:36)

Our more practical lesson from Dusty was that now we always ensure we have the historical vet records on each cat we agree to re-home or take in. We need to know their status and conditions to make the right, responsible choices for the pet. Health conditions are never a reason to turn an animal away in our rescue; we've seen it repeatedly. There *is* a home for every cat. We just need to help them find the right one.

Head bumps and purrs to you, Dusty.

> Blessed are the merciful, for they shall receive mercy. Matthew 5:7

Mick & Zeke

Brotherhood

"To make a difference in someone's life, you don't have to be brilliant, rich, beautiful, or perfect. You just have to care." —Mandy Hale

It was midafternoon when the email, marked urgent, arrived from the local low-cost spay/neuter animal clinic across town. They were imploring me to take in a 16-week-old male, black and white kitten. It was urgent because the vet tech on duty had smuggled him out the clinic's back door to save his life the evening before. Now, he needed a safe place and assistance in finding a permanent home to belong to.

A family had brought him into the clinic requesting that he be euthanized. They were claiming he was too aggressive and specifically did not like men. (*How you would know a 16-week-old baby kitten is aggressive is arguable?*) The family obviously had gotten a kitten, changed their mind, and opted for what they thought was an easier way to release the responsibility. Drop him off and have him put down was their solution. This is an all-too-common issue for pets when owners want to relinquish their responsibilities. They had dropped him off and left promptly, without another word.

In most cases, veterinary personnel would have to secure a release from the 'owners' gaining permission to take possession of the pet in lieu of euthanasia. This family had dumped the kitten and left so quickly there was no time. However, it could cause issues for the clinic if it was known they hadn't complied with the owner's wishes.

This was a stroke of good luck for the kitten. Not only had he escaped the clinic with his life, but he had also escaped a future living with a family where he mattered so little. Now he could be adopted into a much better home. (As for you, you meant evil against me, but God meant it for good, to bring it about that many people should be kept alive, as they are today. Genesis 50:20)

We readily agreed to take him and coordinated his arrival with the clinic technician who had taken him home temporarily. Concern grew after several days had passed and we were still unable to bring him to the rescue. We made arrangements only to have them canceled at the last moment by the vet tech several times.

Perhaps something had changed, or maybe the tech that had taken him home wanted to keep him and just wasn't saying so?

In a last attempt to understand the delay, I called the clinic one last time. As a rescue, every cat we commit to takes up space and resources which are always limited for nonprofit rescues. The result is to turn away other cats in need. This is one of the most heartbreaking, difficult things to do in rescue when your heart wants to help them all.

After waiting over a week, we needed the commitment that this kitten was coming or we would have to move on. I truly did not want this kitten to be let down again and was relieved when we were able to agree on a date and time for him to join us. The vet tech who currently had him would deliver him to us.

She arrived, pulling up to the curb in front of the house. Skipping any type of greeting, she stepped out of the car, reached into the back seat and scruffed the kitten roughly, and sputtered about what an inconvenience he had been. Handing him over with a thrusting motion, she wasted no time climbing back into the car to leave. No carrier, no collar, no way to contain a frightened cat in a stressful situation. *She knew better, leading me to question her choice of profession.* (Cat carriers are always the safest mode of transporting cats to prevent them from darting away and being lost.)

I reached for him with my bare hands, hoping that the lack of aggression the clinic had cited was true. I pulled him in close, cradled him, and walked him toward the Manor as the tech pulled away from the curb. *Good Riddance!*

He was a beautiful 4-month-old kitten, with bright, clear, green eyes. His fur was silky and glossy with the stark contrasts in color of the tuxedo cat. From the deep black jacket across his back, to the bright white accents covering his belly, and up from chest to neck like a perfectly pressed ascot. Continuing up the underside of his chin and muzzle, the white covered one cheek, a little off center, up and over his nose, forming a perfect point mid forehead. All four paws looked as if they'd been dipped in white, finishing his formal tuxedo look with white gloves.

Understandably, he was scared and uncertain about what was happening to him now. Given that he hadn't had the best experiences with humankind it seemed right, making it imperative to ease his stress. I spoke with him in gentle tones, infusing positive energy and hope into my words, so he could let down and experience at least some kindness.

"*It's okay, little one,*" I whispered to him. "*Your life will get better and better from here.*"

"*You can trust us. Once you're a Doodlebug, you're always a Doodlebug. You'll always have somewhere to belong, I promise.*"

That's the promise we make to all our rescue cats: no matter where the future takes them, if they find themselves unhappy or in trouble, they are always welcome back with us.

Placing him in the large dog cage I'd set up for him earlier, he settled squarely on the soft bed in the middle to survey his new surroundings. A sheet covered three quarters of the way around the cage to provide some privacy and a feeling of security and safety for him inside. Leaving the very front of the cage uncovered allowed both him and his new housemates to get acquainted slowly.

We always start our newest cats in a protected area like this to give them time to adjust, relax, and get comfortable in their new surroundings. This also gives the other Doodlebugs in our community a chance to observe and become familiar with the newcomer as part of their environment. The introduction methods used when bringing a new cat into the group are always important. Giving them all a chance to greet, approach, and develop a familiarity puts everyone at ease before we release them to exist free-range together. It also serves as a precaution, allowing us to observe the interactions, avoid any altercations, and address any acts of aggression that might flare up at first.

This kitten was tired, unsure, and dealing with a lot of change in a short time, so once he started settling in, I stayed with him a while, reassuring both him and the other cats. When his eyes could no longer resist the urge to close, I watched him relax into sleep, and quietly left to give him some private down time from my presence.

Knowing he was welcome and wanted here would go a long way to making him feel safe and comfortable, so he could exhale and get a good night's sleep. There is a typical long breath exhaled that occurs once we remove an animal from danger and they realize they are finally safe. It's a kind of decompression sigh, where the tension visibly leaves their body and they are truly at rest, it's beautiful to witness.

I stopped in briefly to check on the cats one more time before lights out for the night. Everyone was doing well. The kitten had sampled some of his food and was once again resting. Everyone else was going about their evening rituals of play or sleep, so I slipped out quietly, to avoid disturbing their tranquility.

The following day, I found them all awake, playing and anxiously awaiting breakfast. Our newest friend was also awake, watching the goings on around him. Noting no signs of stress or aggression from any of the cats, I slowly opened the cage door to let the kitten walk out and begin exploring. I had decided on the name 'Mick' for him, after a character in a popular television series at the time. Both 'Micks' found themselves in a new world requiring great skill to adapt and belong. I wanted the name to bring this kitten success as it had for the character.

I served breakfast in the common area and sat a dish down for each cat. Eating together is an excellent technique to assist in cat bonding. It's a neutral, common area with rewards of food, so cats associate this as a safe, happy place.

Everyone seemed content until one of the smaller kittens, used to sharing with his littermates, poked his head into Mick's plate. Mick growled a low warning, so the kitten beat a hasty retreat to another bowl. Mick had shown his tough exterior to get his bluff in on the kittens, and it had worked. The other kittens took the lesson to heart and didn't intrude.

During the coming days, everyone settled in and things went on as usual inside the Manor. Mick took a liking to the loft area for napping because it provided a wonderful vantage point to watch everything from up high. He was a bit of a loner, but still blended into the group.

To continue improving our rescue environment for the cats, we had arranged for a contractor friend to build a 'catio' onto the existing building under a lovely shade tree, with a cat door for the cats to access at their leisure. It was a nice, enclosed porch allowing the cats some outside time to stretch in the sun or enjoy the evening shade.

On his arrival, Gregg walked the contractor around describing what we had in mind for the catio. Once construction had begun, Gregg called me outside to come see the progress. I was excited, thinking he was referring to the progress on the catio, but there was more. He'd forgotten to warn his friend that we were told Mick might be aggressive toward men, and to be careful. It turned out no warning was necessary. Gregg had walked over to find Mick cradled on our friend's arm, receiving a chin scratch, purring his contentment. Far from being aggressive, Mick seemed to have warmed up to our friend, and preferred being cuddled. Here was proof that Mick had been accused of behavior that would have cost him his life. As he had no voice to refute the accusations, all for the convenience of lazy owners. (Those who are "righteous" and just are kind to their animals, and those who are "wicked" and are cruel to creatures under their care. Genesis 24:19)

Mick stayed with us a little while in the rescue, while some kittens were adopted and new arrivals came in. It was a natural rhythm at the rescue. Mick had a tendency to disappear into the loft when potential adopters came if he was not interested in meeting them. (Proof positive that cats choose their people.) A few potential adopters responded to meet him based on his photos and description, but Mick disappeared each time. This was how he let me know that these potential suitors would not do. Ultimately, the decision of adoption is always left to our cats/kittens to determine.

The arrival of one black 5-week-old kitten (Zeke) and his tabby littermate (Trevor) proved to be the catalyst that changed the course of Mick's life.

By now, Mick was around 6 months old. Still a bit of a loner, but playful when he felt like it. (A quick peek beneath his tough exterior.) Zeke had plans for Mick; he had chosen him to be his new buddy. Zeke followed him, tried to play with him, and would do anything his 5-week-old body could manage in an attempt to win Mick's attention. If Mick did it, Zeke did it too. It surprised us that Zeke preferred spending time with a kitten so much older than himself when his own littermate was there. Theirs was just a friendship meant to be.

Zeke had the heart to see through Mick's tough exterior. He could see past the hurt and fear imprinted in his heart from his former abandonment and the cruelty he'd been subjected to. Zeke saw something much more.

At first, Mick fought hard to hang onto his loner lifestyle, but Zeke remained vigilant in his pursuit of Mick's friendship; he had chosen him to be his new big brother. The protective walls Mick had built were no match for Zeke's determination. The final sign that Mick's resolve was fading was the evening Zeke followed him to the dinner bowls and proudly stuck his head into Mick's. Mick began his low rumble to growl Zeke off. (All the kittens knew this was forbidden.)

Zeke took one step back, looked Mick in the eye, and bent down for another bite! The low rumble began again, but Zeke ignored it and continued to share with Mick. Zeke's perseverance had won out as Mick reluctantly offered him some respect, and accepted Zeke as his new companion. From that point forward, we considered them "Mick and Zeke," a matched set. As they grew closer, it became clear that to respect the bond they'd formed, we would need to adopt them into the same home together

When the email arrived a few weeks later from a couple wanting to adopt a bonded pair of cats, I immediately thought of the boys. Mick's behavior would tell me if this was the home, I'd become accustomed to his habit of disappearing just out of sight in the loft. If these adopters weren't the ones for Mick, we had other kittens waiting for their home. (We always prefer to adopt kittens in pairs anyway.)

On arrival, Zeke and the other kittens greeted the couple, all playful and friendly, pouring out their charm. The couple described how important their pets were to them, and what they were hoping to find in their new cats, but the bonded pair was their topmost wish. Melissa, the lady, had taken a liking to Zeke from our kitten pack. The gentleman, Ferrell, was hoping to find a cat that would really bond with him and be his buddy.

As if on cue, Melissa was asking if Zeke was part of the bonded pair of kittens she'd seen on our placement website. She inquired about his bonded buddy Mick. I explained to them that Mick was his buddy, but that he often hid from visitors. I really wanted them to meet him but it might take some coaxing since Mick was so shy.

As I was relaying this to them, I looked up to see Mick lifting his head and looking down at us from the loft. He slowly stood up, stretched, and casually began winding his way down the stairs. Pausing at the feeding area, he stared openly at our little circle, deciding if he would join us. Walking over to where we were, he looked at us, circled once, and curled up right against Ferrell's back. I was stunned, in a wonderful way, and while Mick sought chin rubs and head butted Ferrell, I expressed my delight, explaining that Mick had never done this with any other potential adopters.

I'd known that Mick would let me know when the right person came along, and this was the clearest indication I'd ever experienced of a cat choosing their person. The decision was so swift, and final, it was amazing to watch this happen. They were both delighted that the kittens had chosen them mutually.

To this day, I believe Mick recognized the need in Ferrell's heart for a friend and confidante. What Zeke had extended to Mick had healed the pain from the past within his heart. Now, Mick was reaching out to a heart that wanted the same friendship built on unconditional love.

I really liked this couple from the start of our meeting, picking up on their kind spirits, and their love for animals. The conversation between us had flowed easily, and they were excited to be taking these two new additions to the family home. It was always a blessing to us as rescuers to know that the animals we loved had found their happily ever after.

The kittens were on their way to their new forever home that afternoon. Mick had been such a presence and a big personality that we missed him for some time in the Manor. But that paled compared to the joy we felt that he and Zeke had found their happily ever after together. They promised to send us updates and pictures so we could share in their new adventure.

The bond of brotherhood that had formed between these two kittens due to Zeke's persistence as a loving, open-hearted kitten is such a beautiful example of the love God wants us to feel for one another. It created such a wonderful, impactful expression of The Golden Rule. (And as you wish that others would do to you, do so to them. Luke 6:31)

Zeke, the innocent baby kitten that he was, instinctively looked past the protective walls (the tough act) Mick put forward to see into his true heart and love him as a brother. In turn, because Zeke had seen the real Mick and loved him through his pain, Mick could identify with Ferrell's heart and loved him for who his heart said he truly was.

The pure loving expression of one heart reaching out to love another set in motion the most incredible real life expression God wants us to follow. (A new commandment I give to you, that you love one another: just as I have loved you, you also are to love one another. John 13:34)

Zeke followed God's plan out of pure love and an open heart, instinctively. Just as God speaks to our hearts, He also leads His animals to care for one another as He cares for them. Zeke began an amazing circle of love that transcended existing emotional barriers and pain to heal and bring together a 'soul family.' Zeke's willingness to love openly and to give of himself opened the door to God's presence and love, which created a much stronger bond to last beyond the earthly ties. Extending even further as we'll see in a later chapter...

Epilogue: Mick and Zeke were truly blessed with the bond they created and the family of which they became a part.

Mick developed cancer in his 6th year, causing us to mourn his loss later that same year. The course of his life had navigated some twists and turns, but we are so grateful for the love and joy his life brought to others. Overcoming abandonment by his original family and the sentence of euthanasia at 16 weeks, he went on to share a life of acceptance and love with a better family. We are grateful to God for the love he brought to all those who took the time to know him, and that he spent his time on Earth as a beloved pet and friend. The impact one little tuxedo kitten had on those of us who knew and loved him is unforgettable.

The chain of love started by one baby kitten continues as Melissa and Ferrell became our dear friends, and they continue to extend that same expression of unselfish love in support of the rescue and their love of animals. We will see them again in a coming chapter.

> My times are in your hands; rescue me from the hand of my enemies and from my persecutors! Psalm 31:15

> So now faith, hope, and love abide, these three; but the greatest of these is love. 1 Corinthians 13:13

Walter the Pigeon

A Lesson in Courage

Bloom where you are planted —Bishop of Geneva, Saint Francis de Sales

The car pulled up beside our driveway and I walked over to greet the young lady and the tiny kitten she had in tow to surrender to our rescue.

As we were getting acquainted, a tall young man stepped out of the car's passenger side to join us. She introduced him as her brother, and there, sitting calmly on his right shoulder, was a pretty gray pigeon!

The bird was unruffled. Its head bobbed slightly, looking around the new environment, perfectly at ease. It showed no interest in giving up its current perch even as we walked together around the house to the backyard where the rescue Manor was positioned.

"Is this your pet?" I asked him, just a little bewildered by his choice to bring a pet bird to a cat rescue? Especially one who was untethered or protected by a lead.

"No," he answered. "I was downtown last night with some friends and this bird flew over and landed on my shoulder. He's been there ever since."

Unsure what to make of that, but intrigued, I forged on.

"He's been with you since last night?" I asked, a little incredulously.

"Yeh," he answered, shrugging his shoulders. "Slept right up there last night, too."

The young man seemed so unfazed by the unusual occurrence I was unsure what to believe. This bird had been with him since last night, along for the car ride to our rescue, and now sitting on his shoulder in the open air, making no attempt to leave.

I questioned whether he was trying to be funny, or if this was real.

His sister confirmed he had indeed shown up with a pigeon on his shoulder the night before and it was still there this morning.

Reaching the Manor, our discussion returned to the kitten.

She explained that since caring for this little kitten for a few days, she'd really grown to love him, and surrendering him was harder than she'd expected. However, she and her husband agreed they were not in the right position to care for a pet right now, and wanted him to have the best care and find his forever home.

Sitting inside the cat carrier nested in a blanket was a tiny, gray tabby kitten. He looked to be about 5 weeks old, still too young to be totally weaned and separated from his mama cat. Since they had found him as a stray on his own, there was little we could do about that, but welcome him into the rescue with the other orphaned babies and care for him until he could be adopted into a loving home.

His little perky ears were the perfect little triangles for a kitten his age, sitting on top of his full forehead. He had a few white markings on his paws and muzzle, and his soft, rounded belly. His huge, round, blue eyes held the innocence of a baby as he looked up at me. He was adorable.

It was always unfortunate to find a tiny one like this separated from his mama, knowing he had missed out on the benefits of the training and attention his mama would provide. More concerning was the loss of colostrum he might've missed from his mother cat. (Feline colostrum is passed to kittens in their mother's milk. Rich in antibodies, it helps to develop immune systems.) This kitten appeared to be alert and a healthy weight. He would blend right into our Doodlebug crew.

We'd reached the front porch of the Manor. I asked the bird's name, and if he felt comfortable walking into a cat rescue environment with an untethered bird on his shoulder, reminding him we were in a non-caged environment.

The young man's response was astounding to me, again delivered nonchalantly. He was not concerned that the bird would be upset or cause any chaos, and no, he hadn't given the bird a name yet.

I was not as convinced about the response we would receive, so we entered the Manor slowly to monitor what was about to happen.

Upon our entry, the bird arched his head and gave a gentle ruffle of his feathers, looked around, but appeared completely content. I watched as the young man casually reached up and rubbed his neck. (I had never witnessed anything like this outside of a Cinderella movie!)

Turning my attention back to the kitten, we introduced him to the new environment, watching as he explored for a few moments. There was so much to see for such a tiny guy, so many toys and nooks, other kittens and larger cats peering at him from the sleeping loft above. Our rescue cats were used to newcomers and might give him a sniff, but few of them would give up their nap time to investigate. There was time for all of that.

We tucked him into a soft blanket on a cat bed in the corner so he could relax and observe his new surroundings but feel safe and protected. This was a lot for such a tiny one to take in all at once. As he snuggled down into the blanket and his eyes closed, we quietly stepped back out the door and onto the porch.

The air was alive with the music from an orchestra of birds calling to one another. Their happy chatter filled the trees with the sound of nature. The hickory and other tree species were in full bloom, creating a protective canopy and cooling shade overhead, while the privacy fence that hugged the back corner of the yard there created a safe and inviting corner for our bird neighbors.

We kept a tray of wild bird seed on the top of the wide porch rails for the birds to help themselves as we enjoyed watching them. We had a wide variety of birds native to Tennessee, including robins, blue jays, cardinals, sparrows, and even an occasional woodpecker, but I'd never seen a pigeon this far into the suburbs.

Pausing beside the tray for a moment, the young man scooped a bit of seed into his hand and held it out for our new pigeon friend. We were all interested to see if any of this would sway the bird to leave his perch on the young man's shoulder, perhaps the large tray of seed would be the temptation that lured him over, but no. He accepted the offering from the outstretched hand but remained where he was.

As we continued through the yard, a small grouping of birds swooped down onto the neighbor's roof, chirped back and forth, then took flight again, chasing one another and disappearing into trees above.

It was then, with a gentle flurry of wings, the pigeon launched himself up, and flew from the young man's shoulder over to the neighbor's roof! He sat there surveying what he could see from this new vantage point across rooftops and trees and into the open blue sky. I imagine it was quite a different view from that of the city he was accustomed to.

Standing there for a few moments, we observed his movements, watching and wondering *"might he still return to the young man's shoulder?"* Or would he choose to take a chance on this new opportunity away from the city noise, smog, and pecking sidewalks for food scraps. Scurrying to avoid crowds on the sidewalks or traffic in the streets. (City bird, country bird?)

When it appeared he was perched on the roof with no intention of moving, we continued on the way back to their car. Was there still a chance that seeing the young man leave, he might fly over to join him again? But no; we exchanged goodbyes and as the car drove off, I could still see the pigeon on the rooftop.

I walked back to the rescue to check on the new kitten and spend some time with the cats, sending a welcoming greeting to our new bird neighbor as I passed by.

That afternoon, I shared the unusual story with Gregg, pointing out the bird on our neighbor's roof. We kept an eye on him as evening approached. Still in the same relative position on the same roof, the pigeon never moved, even as other birds flew nearby and rustled in the trees.

Well, it appeared he was here to stay, at least for a while, so we offered him a proper name. Walter, he would be Walter Pigeon.

Just before nightfall, Walter took his first steps, gliding down the roof and hopping onto the fence top. Still observant, he hopped a few steps further along the fence, making his way toward the seed tray. He stopped to nibble a few bites from the tray and to take a closer look around, then with a gentle flapping of his wings, he disappeared into the trees.

Watching for him the next day, we witnessed Walter's return to the yard, hopping along on the fence like an old routine now. I wondered if he'd chosen his new home in the trees and settled in. He was the only pigeon among the flock of birds in the yard, making him easy to spot on his visits. We continued to follow the saga of our city turned country bird, always glad to see him.

Less than a week later, the young lady who had brought the kitten to us originally contacted me about coming to take him home. She and her husband had missed caring for the little guy so much she called to ask if it would be possible to return to take him home with her to keep. And so, our newest Doodlebug returned with the people who had found him, to his happily ever after.

Over time, we became accustomed to seeing Walter among the bird community in our trees. Swooping, perching, and sometimes walking the fence. We considered him an honorary Doodlebug and enjoyed knowing he was here, happy, and free.

The following spring, Walter appeared again on the fence, hopping and dancing, only this time he had a friend. She was a smaller bird, in a deeper shade of solid gray. It appeared Walter had found a mate. She hopped along with him, then they flew off into the trees.

We often wondered if he'd met another pigeon here, perhaps another city turned country pigeon? Or had he known her in the city, was this his mate and he'd gone back to get her and bring her here? Either way, it was wonderful to see Walter building a life along with Wilma. (We dubbed Walter's significant other 'Wilma' and would enjoy spotting them in the yard and flying about.)

Later that spring, we were blessed to see our happy twosome had blossomed into a threesome with the appearance of a baby pigeon in tow. It was inspiring, and wonderful to watch their story unfold, and be a part of it somehow.

I believe, to this day, the birds playing and swooping through the trees and over the roof were calling to Walter that first day with an excited energy, and exhibiting a freedom that city birds just don't experience. I believe it was a 'welcome to the neighborhood' greeting. That invitation to stay, along with the birdseed and the canopy of trees against the open sky was too much to resist compared to his old lifestyle.

This bird had taken a chance by landing on a man's shoulder, and riding it to a whole new adventure in the unknown. Then, as quickly as he'd decided to leave the city, he'd decided to stay here where he had landed and grow.

Walter's story exemplifies the expression of courage and strength in what would've been a frightening journey for a small bird on his own. Yet he persevered and was all the better for it in the end. What would lead a bird against all instincts into a house of his enemies? Walter knew something instinctively that I have found through my faith in God.

Often, when we find ourselves in frightening or strange situations, it's tempting to think that God is apart from us. We can let our fear and anxiety rule our heart when God is always with us. (Be strong and courageous. Do not fear or be in dread of them, for it is the LORD your God who goes with you. He will not leave you or forsake you. Deuteronomy 31:6) Trust in him and he will always lead us to the best outcome.

I often think of the little family of pigeons living their best life in the suburbs, and our unusual meeting. Meeting Walter and caring for him as our accidental rescue bird was an unexpected blessing for us indeed.

> Have I not commanded you? Be strong and courageous. Do not be frightened, and do not be dismayed, for the LORD your God is with you wherever you go. Joshua 1:9
>
> Are not five sparrows sold for two pennies? And not one of them is forgotten before God. Luke 12:6

Friskie

My Gentle Companion

"Do not go where the path may lead, go instead where there is no path and leave a trail."

—Ralph Waldo Emerson

A 2200 sq. ft. red brick two-story surrounded by lush green grass on a private half acre yard with native hickory trees and 15 or so feral kitties, the last of these were not on our list of 'must haves' for our newly purchased homestead.

We assume they were already there and had been through a few generations, but there is the *possibility* that the word was out on us from other cats, (yes, they do talk to each other,) and the cats found us!

Our neighbor cats resided in the ditch between our backyard fence and the road. Before the expansion of homes and communities in the area, this was a small rural road with little traffic. Along with the rapid development came a measurable increase in traffic.

After moving into the house, it hadn't taken very long to discover the colony. Our dog Joey, the world's most animal friendly black Lab, had picked up their scent. He looked at the fence, then sniffed excitedly all around the bottom whining. Peeking over the top, we could just make out the outline of a cat sitting in the shade of a tree, semi-covered by brush and low-lying branches. Soon after that, he'd spotted some tiny kitten noses peeking under the fence where there was a gap between the fence bottom and the ground. Just a few inches, but large enough for the kittens to wiggle through.

We were no strangers to working with feral cats. Josie and the feral cats in our last neighborhood had taught us well. We set up a feral cat feeding station, added a nice cedarwood pet house complete with a shingled roof and a small front porch. All of it was nestled in the back corner of the yard where the fence formed a protected area underneath a small grouping of shade trees.

Through the next several seasons, we worked to trap, neuter, and rehome (TNR) this colony of cats/kittens. As before, we found the cats were not all feral but contained a mix including abandoned, lost, and an occasional 'escapee' who had found their way out of the house for a couple days to explore before they made their way back home. It was slow and steady work, focused on spay/neuter, socializing, and placement. For those who would socialize, we found indoor homes. Those who were better suited to the life of a working cat (by choice) we found barn homes and farm placements. A few of the cats were even adopted by the local Lowe's and Home Depot locations where they were cared for as a pet but lived in the warehouses to work as rodent control. Whichever lifestyle suited each cat, they all held the promise of better lives than what was awaiting them as outdoor cats along that ditch. For a few of the older cats who would not be socialized, we would trap, perform TNR, including the ear tip, and then release them back to the ditch. (Ear tipping is a standard process where the very tip of a cat's ear is clipped to indicate they are altered when they are to be released back outdoors.) We always provided support and maintained the little colony that remained feral.

Each year, new kittens peeking through or wiggling underneath the bottom of the fence would mark the arrival of spring. The Queens would set up their nesting area just on the other side of the fence, close to the feral station. Once in a while, in the early mornings or just after sunset, the outline of an adult cat could be seen there. Once the kittens were weaned and old enough to eat solid food, they'd appear. The number of cats we'd successfully rehomed from the colony was growing while diminishing the numbers still repeating the cycle of feral births within the ditch. This was a comfortable pattern we'd fallen into with the cats, and it was a successful process. We were content to continue on in the same way until the colony had been homed or completely spayed/neutered.

That is until the evening I met Friskie.

Stepping outside to water the front landscaping in the early evening was a ritual I enjoyed. Southern summers are hot and without a little extra support through the driest parts, flowers wither, lawns become brown and crunchy, and the trees can wilt. I enjoyed a few uninterrupted prayer times among the beauty of God's nature. A few minutes to speak with God about the day and feel His restful, restorative peace.

I completed the watering and heading over to replace the hose, caught a movement out of the corner of my eye. Something small appeared to be bobbing in and out of the storm drain centered on the street in front of our house. Crossing the lawn to gain a better look, I spotted two little orange ears popping up and down, followed by the top of a small furry head. Next, there was a quick reflection from two little eyes that disappeared back into the drain as soon as they had appeared. The little head appeared again, followed by another set of ears poking up over the edge of the rain gutter.

Well, this was new.

Two kittens, not more than 8–10 weeks old, were playing in the storm drain! Whether they were chasing one another or the leaves that had drifted into the drain, they were having a wonderful time. One set of ears was an unmistakably orange tabby. The second set was a warm brown with a smokey quality, similar to the markings on a Siamese.

I stayed there a while, watching the kittens quietly from my position in the front yard to see what I could find out by observing. The adult cats of the neighborhood used the storm drain system as a makeshift subway. We observed them emerging from and disappearing back into the rain gutters on their travels through the community. This was sensible, as it provided cover to allow them to move about in a more discreet manner. These kittens were considerably younger.

How many kittens were there? Where did they come from? Were they a part of the backyard colony, or where did they belong? How did they come to be here? Were they lost? Was there a Mama cat who would come to gather them and take them home?

There are many stories on the local news, social media, or documentaries showing kittens trapped inside the drains or swept away when heavy rains fill them to overflowing. There could be more, including any that might get injured or stuck. It was dry now, but Tennessee went from drought-like conditions to torrential downpours, causing flash flooding in many areas.

One thing was sure, the storm drains were not a safe place for kittens.

The plan of rescue for these two kittens formed in my mind. It would require a little fine-tuning compared to our usual tried & true set up in the backyard.

The evening was giving way to nightfall now as the light dimmed and the faint outline of the moon was becoming visible. It wouldn't be long now until the silky blackness of night settled in. The kittens were still here, playing. They were curious, but hadn't mustered the courage yet to step outside the drain to investigate further. Doing so would place them squarely on the road and in imminent danger from passing cars. They seemed to have the fear instinct and would retreat at the sound of an engine or the bright headlights. This was encouraging.

I stepped quickly to gather the things I needed (a 'rescue kitten' kit) to set up a little camp in my front yard near enough to entice them out of the drain and bring them to safety. The best approach with feral or outdoor cats is to simply be a part of their environment at first so that they will accept you there. (The term "herding feral cats" is a real thing!) The trick is to give them time to feel comfortable and slowly interact in order to earn their trust.

This is never an instant process; patience and endurance are the keys. This became my evening ritual for the next few nights. We began with a plate of wet food placed right at the opening of the storm drain to get their attention. Then, for hours, I would sit quietly and dangle the wand toy (ripped up stretchy strips of T-shirts on dowel rods) within reach of the kittens; as they gained courage in chasing the 'prey,' I would pull the toy farther and farther out of the drain. The more intrigued they became, the closer they would advance toward where I sat. Next, I spoke in soothing, light tones to acquaint them with my voice.

Each time at the end of the evening together, I would leave a small trail of treats from the drain into the front yard to another small bowl of food in front of where I sat. Each evening, they became more comfortable and adventurous, wandering further up onto the grass. They became so engrossed in playing that they forgot their inhibitions and would throw themselves into it or grab on so tight to the rag that they wouldn't let go. Now they were at ease playing, and I could pet them gently. The next move was to scoop them up and into safety within the rescue.

The little orange tabby, now called Friskie, was touch-friendly, and was able to be picked up. I had him in my arms and walked quickly to the rescue building, sitting him down, and speaking to him the entire time. Friskie was a mixed tabby, with mostly orange fur, the traditional ringed tail, with mixes of white fur on his face and belly. The more outgoing of the two kittens, he was still uneasy in this new environment. His curiosity won out as he hopped up onto the top of the kitty condo nearest the window. Perched there, he appeared more content to stare out the window at the view. I suspect he was searching for his brother.

I'd returned to the front storm drain to see what the chances were of repeating this with Frankie. Frankie was a beige, medium-haired kitten with those smokey tips on his ears and a matching mask like a Siamese with startlingly beautiful blue eyes. He was the more timid of the two kittens and was accustomed to following Friskie's lead.

This might work in my favor if he will let me pick him up and take him to be with his brother; or it could make catching him harder if he'd been frightened at seeing Friskie taken off and finding himself alone.

When I returned, it was just in time to see Frankie's tail disappear into the grate. I hated to leave Frankie out there on his own, but it was part of getting them inside and safely into the rescue. I prayed God would watch over Frankie, protect him and ease any fear or sadness he was feeling without his brother there at his side. I also prayed God would guide me to the best approach to catch Frankie so the two brothers could be reunited.

To my relief, Frankie returned the next day, and we resumed our routine of play as I continued to work with him, talking and telling him Friskie was waiting for him inside the rescue, safe and sound, as he could be too. (And praying God would touch his heart and allow me to take him inside.)

Meanwhile, Friskie hated being inside the rescue for his first few days. He sat in the same window, looking out vigilantly, watching for his brother. There were other kittens in the rescue he could play and eat with. He was okay with my petting him and trying to soothe him, but he was not happy. He remained in the window. Meanwhile, my attempts to gather Frankie and reunite them remained a work in progress.

Speaking to Friskie, I sat with him and tried to settle him in. I told him about the differences between being an outside kitty and indoor kitty. Outside, he was exposed to the elements and dangers of outdoor life. Being inside, he would have food and shelter, and look forward to being adopted by someone who would love him.

It soon became clear that my efforts were of no use; he was unhappy. Some cats are just not satisfied with a totally indoor existence. Although there are dangers and they risk shorter lives existing as outdoor cats, sometimes it comes down to the quality of their life over the quantity.

That evening, I reluctantly told Friskie that if he was still this unhappy in the AM, I would release him back to the front yard drain to be with his brother. (I would, of course, trap them later when they were old enough to ensure I vetted them.) I'd have to accept his choice and be prepared to maintain them as outdoor kitties.He was told the decision was his. If he chose to be outside, I would respect it, but my heart silently broke a little.

The next morning, nothing had changed. Friskie was still unhappy. It was with resignation I returned him to the front yard by the storm grate to find his brother. I held the hope in my heart that perhaps Friskie would find his brother and lead him back to us.

Walking alongside Friskie to the front yard, I refilled the water and food bowls I'd left out for Frankie. Glancing around just in case, but there was no sign of him.

Then I watched as Friskie disappeared down the storm drain.

I went about the rest of my day feeling sad and a little defeated. It was one of the hardest things I'd ever done in the rescue, and I worried about him. I prayed for blessings over both cats and that God would watch over them and keep them safe. I prayed God would grant us the gift of both cats coming back together. In my heart, I was convinced I'd done right by Friskie, given the circumstances. He'd told me his choice, and I respected it. Still, it wasn't what I'd hoped for him. I asked God to forgive me if I'd failed in rescuing these sweet boys and to please show me the answer.

That evening after work, walking from the car up the driveway, I glanced over at the storm drain just in case, then crossed to the front yard. There was no sign of Frankie, but there, looking right at me, was Friskie! It looked as if he'd been waiting for me. It thrilled me to see him and to see he was fine.

As I called out to him, he looked directly at me. He responded with a tiny 'mew' and came right over to me in a little cat trot. (Slightly more speed than the usual gate of a cat.) His tail held high, he wound his body around my legs in greeting and applied head bumps. He was happy to see me, too.

Reaching down to pick him up, I embraced him in a hug.

"I'm glad to see you, buddy," I told him.

I continued to hug him, carrying him as we walked back to the rescue. Opening the front door, I sat him back down on the porch so he could see inside. The choice had to be his own, and knowing I couldn't bear to face releasing him again, I looked at him and whispered,

"Be sure." I'd love to bring you inside and know you're safe, but this is a final decision to be an inside kitty."

At that, he looked at me, paused to look behind him for a moment, and stepped inside the rescue, making himself at home. I was elated. Friskie was home.

I'd been consistent in putting out food and water for Frankie, watching for him to see that he came each evening and was doing okay. We had developed enough of a bond by this time that he would come over to eat beside me, and I could pat him, but at any unfamiliar movement he would bolt. We'd established our terms of friendship for now. Frankie would probably need to be trapped and brought in to settle into the rescue. (Trapping him at this point would feel like a violation of our terms, but it was for his sake, and it would need to be done.)

Once again, I was following the routine, refilling the food and water station, when I opened the front screen door to step outside. With my arms full, I turned sideways to slide through the opening. When, in a quick instant, I saw something white push past me and dart into the house, just as the screen door snapped shut.

Frankie's curiosity had gotten the best of him! There he stood on the inside, looking out at me! When the screen had snapped shut, it pushed his backend the rest of the way into the house, effectively trapping him inside! I looked up to see him peering back at me, a little bewildered. Both of us in a momentary pause as we realized what had just transpired.

Blinking for a moment, I absorbed this ironic twist, then wasting no time, I darted around the side of the house to the back door, calling to Gregg to come meet me with a cat carrier. Carefully opening the back patio door to return inside, I slowly advanced behind him, closing the main door slowly, gently until he was wedged between the open front door and closed screen, leaving only a slim escape route. Right in front of that escape route, Gregg had placed the carrier with the door open and stood behind it. With only one direction he could move, Frankie ran toward the open carrier and right inside. I stood for the briefest of moments, realizing what had just taken place, then exhaled.

If it hadn't been for prayer, I'd never have known what prompted him to be brave enough to poke his head inside the door that day.

Was it to see where I went each time I left? Was it to see if this was where Friskie had gone? Did something interest him from inside the house?

All I really know to this day is that it was not only the answer to my prayer, it was God granting me an outcome far beyond what I'd even dreamed to ask. I had asked God for the answer, and here it was and more. I believe to this day, God granted Frankie the courage within his heart to come inside that day to a better life.

Frankie and I made the trip to the rescue building and carefully I sat the carrier on the floor facing out for him to spot Friskie. When I opened the door, Friskie immediately poked his head inside to escort Frankie out and welcome him.

Happy to be reunited, it wasn't long until the brothers became settled in contentedly as part of our Doodlebug Manor family. Life would be easier and much better from here.

It's never easy in rescue to predetermine which kittens will be adopted, when, and by whom. The bonds that hold younger kittens and siblings together sometimes diminish as they grow up and take on the traits of independence found in adult cats. Over some time, this had been the case for these two brothers.

Frankie was a very appealing, beautiful kitten with those bright blue eyes and a graceful stance that had many admirers. His forever family had come all the way from West Virginia to meet him upon seeing his picture posted on our adoption site. He so resembled a special cat the father had had and adored growing up that once they met him and experienced his calm, easygoing demeanor, they immediately adopted him.

Frankie had gone home with his family, while Friskie remained with us at the Manor. He continued to be an outgoing, even-tempered boy who loved to explore and play with the kittens.

My bond with Friskie grew stronger over time as he remained at the Manor. He was a popular fellow and would soon turn a year old.

Friskie was a sweet, laid-back cat, loved the play corner in the Manor, and lounging on the cat condo beside the window. He was happy to be on the catio or napping in the loft and would always greet me with a tail twitch when I entered the Manor. He was a master of contentment.

Truthfully, Friskie had never totally given up his love of the outdoors. When I would work in the rescue garden, or he could see leaves blowing past him from his position on the catio, he wanted to be a part of it. He still enjoyed the feel of the breeze on his face, sitting on the warm front porch surveying the yard, or investigating underneath the plant leaves in the garden,

Eventually, I gave in to his yearning for a little outside time. Our yard was surrounded by an 8-foot privacy fence, catnip in the garden, and excellent shade from the tall trees. But he spent most of his time outside with me lounging on the front porch of the rescue, nestled on the warm wooden planks between the pots of flowers and plants. He would sit there as often as he could outside and always tip his face toward the sun in perfect contentment.

A random picture of him captured one afternoon in his favorite spot on the porch, face basking in the sun, was so charming that it became the logo for the rescue. Even today, he is the face of Doodlebug Manor.

Through his seniority at the rescue and his fantastic manner with the kittens, Friskie had assumed a role as a sort of den father. I viewed him as a gentle, happy companion and friend.

Shortly after turning a year old, Friskie was adopted along with one of his rescue kitten brothers, Luca, into a beautiful sunny ranch-style home with plenty of room to lie in the warm sun. While his adoptive mother laughed at the notion of his name (Friskie had matured and no longer retained the wild energy of his kittenhood) she loved him and his brother greatly. They had found their wonderful indoor home.

We are thankful daily that God has chosen us to work with His animals. It's a blessing to have the opportunity to help and fall in love with all these amazing souls who love unconditionally and shine as an example of God's love in our world.

Sometimes God may call us to perform in a way that takes us outside of our comfort zone. When God presents us with challenges where our 'tried and true' methods fail, we are always able to seek His guidance and open our hearts to His teaching. Rather than struggling and trying to do it on our own, as if trying to impress God with our efforts, we can reach out for the answer and God will provide the way. (The Lord is near to all who call on him, to all who call on him in truth. Psalm 145:18)

At the point I felt most discouraged and defeated trying to know the right thing to do for Friskie (Indoor or Outdoor?), God showed me to listen to Friskies heart to find the answer.

When I felt I'd failed completely helping Frankie and had lost hope of catching him, I prayed; *"please God, show me the answer."*

In response, God not only showed me the answer, but presented it. He went beyond what I knew to ask for and delivered Frankie into his future.

If I hadn't known to pray and ask God for the right path to pursue and tried to force the results from my knowledge, the outcome for both boys might have been very different.

We are thankful for God's guidance and love in every challenge we face in working with His animals.

> Ask, and it will be given to you; seek, and you will find; knock, and it will be opened to you. For everyone who asks receives, and the one who seeks finds; and to the one who knocks it will be opened. Matthew 7:7–8

> Trust in the Lord with all your heart, and do not lean on your own understanding. In all your ways acknowledge Him, and He will make straight your paths. Proverbs 3:5-6

Xenia

The Patient Warrior

"Saving one animal won't change the world, but it will change the world for that one animal." —Nathan Winograd

"They are gonna shred my window screens?!" Her voice went up at the end of the sentence as if to signify a question.

"Is this Doodlebug Manor!?" she demanded on the other end of the phone. I must have paused longer than I realized to gather my thoughts.

"Yes, yes, it is," I said confusedly. "Who am I speaking with please?"

She began speaking immediately in a strange tone that wavered between oddly calm and anxious, followed by a strange intermingling of giggling.

"Oh boy," I thought, "here we go." Many rescues, including ours, purposely don't publish their phone number publicly to avoid being blindsided by the number of odd phone calls we are subject to. We prefer contact via social media FIRST to understand inquiries then, follow up with a phone call as needed, allowing us to understand the situation ahead of time.

"How did she get this number?" was my second thought.

However, there was no time to inquire as she continued speaking. It was difficult to understand what she was trying to say amid the unusual cadence of her speech and the non-continuity of her thoughts. Was this related to an emergency animal situation? An inquiry to take in kittens or cats? Or a crank call? It took some effort to decipher but finally I understood that three tiny kittens were found outside.

These kittens were nestled underneath the shrubs below the front window of her condo. She discovered them in response to their loud, insistent cries for help. She decided to contact a cat rescue for assistance when they climbed the screens of her front window in their attempt to find safety and protection. I questioned her briefly to learn what I could about the situation.

Had she seen the mama cat near the location? How old were the babies? Had she tried to catch them or feed them? How long had they been there? Was there any immediate danger she could see, like a neighborhood dog bothering them?

Her responses revealed very little, other than she hadn't seen an adult cat around, nor tried to approach the kittens to check on them. The one perfectly clear thing was her concern over the window screens being damaged, and that the Condo Board might take notice and cause her grief. (This was not going to be easy. Obviously, the priority for her were the window screens, and not the tiny lives reaching out for help underneath her window.)

There wasn't much else I could learn about the situation or their condition until I could get to them. It was late, and her location was far enough away that I wouldn't be able to reach the kittens until the next day. I assured her that Doodlebug Manor would take the kittens and we arranged to meet at a midway point early the next morning.

In the meantime, I urged her to bring them inside for the night to ensure their safety, stressing to her the dangers these little ones faced outside in the dark, alone without the warmth and protection of their mama. To appeal to her concerns, I added that bringing them inside would also prevent any further damage to her screens.

We walked through the process of bringing them in overnight and keeping them in a spare bathroom. A couple of old towels, a makeshift litter pan (aluminum roasting pan or shoe box) and water would keep them safe overnight without too much fuss. There was no way to know the last time they'd eaten, or if they were even old enough for solid food, so I asked her to pick up some premade kitten formula at the store and a can of food to offer them overnight. I would gladly reimburse her for any expense the next day. I emphasized that one overnight stay for 3 small kittens in a bathroom would not be much of a bother and could save their lives. She would then have them inside and they would be easy to gather to bring with her to our meeting in the morning.

There are always so many dangers for kittens outside alone, but this year we were experiencing a large influx of coyotes in the suburban areas. They had been spotted walking down the center of the community streets at night and by the side of the highways. Additionally, there were foxes, and other animals looking to feed their own young. These babies had little chance of surviving outside on their own.

My anxiety was escalating for these babies. I offered up a prayer asking God to protect them and ease their fears. I asked the Lord to guard their hearts and hold them in His protection, to provide for them through the night. (We really had no idea if they were old enough to survive without their Mama kitty for a few hours, never mind the entire night) I prayed He would touch the heart of this lady and convince her to bring them safely inside for the night.

The next morning, I received a followup call from the lady again. Confirming our meeting place and time, she shared with me that when she'd stepped outside to gather them, there was one kitten left.

"Something must've dragged the others off, but this last one was still there." She said with that distorted giggle again.

Outside? She had made no attempt to bring the kittens in overnight, despite my urgent requests. She'd ignored them and left them on their own, ignoring their cries for help. She had done nothing, not even the simplest thing, and the kittens had paid the price for her carelessness with their lives.

What had the remaining kitten been through, left on her own all night? Who knows what she'd been exposed to. Had she seen what happened to her siblings? Had she then been there all night in terror?

Standing breathless for a moment, a wave of nausea hit me, followed by a white-hot rage rising to the surface. Pausing to collect myself, willfully calming my voice, I asked her to double check the area in case the others were there but had wandered. (Or a worse fate, I was thinking.)

How could she have left them outside on their own despite my numerous pleas with her to bring them in? I couldn't decide what was worse, her laissez-faire attitude about what had happened, or her giggling?

The situation was deteriorating quickly. I knew my approach to rescue this kitten successfully would need to include decorum and patience to gain custody. Knowing it was imperative to remain calm and try to conclude our business without letting my own opinions escalate the situation. (Maintaining a cool head when working through the absurdity of some rescue situations with difficult people can be a real challenge, but it is always in the animal's best interest. Removing them from the case and into safety is the first objective.) Too often animals pay the price in rescue situations. This little one had already paid a price, no need to add to her sorrows.

Perhaps the reality wasn't as bad as my mind kept replaying. Perhaps Mama cat had come back to get her babies after all and had run out of time to get this last little one before the lady scooped her up?

I wondered how much of the story she shared was even the truth. Accepting I'd never know the real complete story, it didn't matter as long as the kitten was safe.

Arriving at our destination, I steered us quickly through the greetings, eager to take possession of the kitten and place her safely in our car. Gregg waited behind the steering wheel while I secured her inside the car. Tucking her into a secure carrier, lined with soft warm blankets, I buckled her into the back seat. Knowing the kitten was safe now was what mattered. I did a quick triage of her condition, a girl! Seeing no signs of illness or infections and no signs of injury, we were ready to go.

As we prepared to leave, the woman chatted on, recounting the story of what had happened. I'll never really know, as her words fell on deaf ears. I thanked her for bringing the kitten to us, and closing the door, we drove off.

Arriving back at Doodlebug Manor, I carried the kitten inside and opened the carrier to let her out. I held her, looking her over to better assess her condition, while I welcomed her with happy, encouraging words.

The kitten was a beautiful black & white tuxedo female, around 5–6 weeks old, with large blue kitten eyes, bright and intelligent. She didn't behave as a feral kitten or show any fear. Immediately, she showed an interest in her surroundings and the other kittens around her. Distracted by a few other kittens playing in the toy corner, she headed in their direction. She was friendly and lively, diving into the fun with other kittens. We would soon discover her love of adventure and exploration and how she approached everything with a zest for life. I pointed out the feeding station to her, ensuring she knew where the food and water were, and left her to explore more.

Things were off to a great start. Not knowing the situation before taking in a cat or kitten carries inherent risk. We are never 100% sure what we're committing to until we can meet the feline to determine if they are sick, injured, or suffer behavioral issues. Either way, once we've committed, we see them through all problems. This little girl was vivacious and joyful, she was a blessing.

The name for this baby came easily: Xenia seemed to be a perfect fit. Named after the warrior princess in folklore, with a dark past, who sets out to redeem herself and fight for good. At the time, we didn't know how prophetic this would be!

Xenia aced her initial vet checkup, proving to be a healthy kitten, and we were so glad, given her humble beginnings. Her arrival was a matter of great timing, as we had several other kittens of similar age at the Manor, so she would have friends and other kittens to learn from and grow with. I was glad she would have all these fellow kittens to bond with. It might not replace the siblings she'd lost, but it was an excellent substitute for what we couldn't replace.

An adorable friendship blossomed among the gang in the Manor. So many of the kittens had arrived solo that season, and they seemed to gravitate to one another. Xenia (living up to her namesake) became the unofficial leader of this kitten crew. She was always up to some harmless mischief with a twinkle in her eye. (This rescue season is still one I look back on fondly, due to the bond between the cats. It was a terrific group that included everyone, oldest to youngest.) The core members of her pack were Willow, Weston, and Isabella.

As adoption seasons go, this one was a little slower than previous years. It wasn't uncommon to have ebb and flow in the spring adoption seasons, this year had just started off slower than some but little by little a few of the older kittens in the group found their homes, and others were welcomed into the Manor in their place.

Isabella was a sleek and demure short, black-haired kitten, who had been a big sister of sorts to the younger crowd. She was adopted at about six months old and while we were delighted to see her find her forever home; it marked the beginning of the end of that season's tight knit little group.

Next, Weston, the brownish tabby with a sweet temperament and dashing face, was adopted into his new home as a second kitten. He would have a brother cat to go home to. Weston's adoption left just the two girls, Xenia and Willow, from the original pack. These two were the last of the original spring group still with us in the Manor and they were well bonded. Generally, littermates bond during the early weeks of life. Kittens crave playmates, so even if you adopt kittens from separate litters, they will likely become friends quickly. Most kittens learn social skills by interacting and playing and do quite well together. In contrast, it can take adult, non-sibling cats eight to 12 months to develop bonds.Many times, these bonds built as adults last a lifetime. (See Cagney & Lacey).

The subsequent adoption was Willow. She was a timid girl, with soft, snow-white fur, and huge green eyes. Willow joined her new home as a second kitten to her new big brother and was on her way to a happily ever after. We had tried to get the two girls adopted together, even asking Willows' adopters if they would consider taking Xenia and Willow together due to their bond, but it wasn't the right fit for their family. We were happy for Willow. The follow up pictures sent by her family showed her to be a happy, well-adjusted kitten.

This left Xenia.

My heart broke just a little for Xenia. It felt like the second time her littermates and friends had been removed from her. She was a wonderful kitten, with a lot to give the family who would adopt her. It was difficult to understand why someone hadn't snatched up this little gem. We took comfort in knowing that the right person for the right cat is important and some happily ever afters take a little longer than others. Reminding myself God does all things in his time, I continued to reassure her that her time was coming. I offered a prayer for Xenia that God would hold her heart and fill her with peace and security until her happily ever after came.

Xenia carried on in her usual happy manner. I'm sure she missed her former bonded playmates, but it never showed as she continued onto new adventures and welcomed the new kittens. She was secure and happy at the Manor, which was worth a lot.

Xenia's day arrived when a father and his young daughter came to meet her. The little girl wanted her first kitten and had picked Xenia out from her pictures and profile on our adoption page.

During their visit, we went through the normal process for adoption. Ours includes submitting and reviewing our application ahead of time, an appointment with us to meet the kitten/cat(s), and some vital check points before we agree to adopt. Upon agreement to adopt, we have a contract stipulating several points of understanding with the adopters, mostly about their routine care, our contact information for questions or issues that may come up are included, and the stipulation that if for some reason the adoption doesn't work out they return our cat(s) to us. (Once a Doodlebug, always a Doodlebug!)

Meeting in person also allows us to observe how the potential adopters interact with the cats, and, equally importantly, gauge how the cats react to the potential adopter. (As we know, cats choose their people!) Sometimes the rescue determines the adopters are not the right fit and must say no. There are many fascinating stories we can share on these alone! (See our story Cats Come First.) Our final decisions are always based on the response sent by God to answer our prayers about each cat.

The fact that they had arrived without a carrier when they were planning to adopt a cat gave me pause, but as first-time cat adopters, we'd seen this before and it didn't amount to a red flag despite our instructions to bring one.

While I waited with Xenia for them to get a carrier from the pet store just up the road, I reviewed everything we'd covered and still felt uncomfortable. I wasn't totally convinced this was the right situation for Xenia. But I assured myself this was Xenia's chance to begin her happily ever after and dismissed my doubt. There was nothing solid I could object to. This was why we did what we did. This kitten had survived against ridiculous odds and now she had a home! It seemed Xenia's day had arrived!

Xenia left that day to start her new life, and I prayed then, as I always do, I had made the right decision, that she would have a happy, blessed life.

When our Doodlebugs leave, we take a moment and share with them that they are loved, and they take a tiny piece of my heart with them. We remind them they have been raised with love and taught the kind of behavior to expect from their adopters. They will always be loved. If they find themselves in trouble or need anywhere down the line, they are always welcome to come back. (We follow up with all adopters as needed post adoption to ensure things are going well and answer any questions.)

With Xenia on her way to her new life, the last of that special pack of kittens were home. It felt like a special chapter had ended.

A couple months had passed since Xenia's adoption and we were busy, as always, with the intake and adoptions of the cats we were blessed to care for. Our last report was that Xenia was doing well in her home and we'd counted that adoption as a success.

We were at a point where we had recently adopted our last Doodlebug of the season and were planning to take a break from rescue and a vacation to Europe. Having all our cats adopted worked out well so we wouldn't have to worry about them while we were so far away.

We'd been rescuing for several years, without a complete break in the action, and needed the time to rest and recharge. One of the main reasons many rescues don't last long, or their quality of care provided to the animals declines, is burnout, commonly referred to as 'Compassion Fatigue.'

Compassion fatigue is a condition which stems from repeated exposure to traumatic events and can cause a person to grow numb to situations that would otherwise affect them profoundly. It can be characterized by emotional and physical exhaustion, leading to a diminished ability to empathize or feel compassion for others. It's often described as the negative cost of caring, or secondary traumatic stress.

While it can affect people across the scope of "Care Workers" from Veterinary professionals, rescuers and shelter workers to professionals in human care as well. Rescuers are very much at risk for developing compassion fatigue. It can be a serious condition if left untreated.

While finalizing our plans just a couple of days before departure, I received an upsetting email addressed to the rescue. Apparently, a former adopter was proposing the ultimatum that he would drop off our former Doodlebug at the county "High Kill" shelter if he didn't hear back from us by the next couple of days.

I recognized the name. This was Xenia's adopter!

Considering we had provided all our contact information and reached out to him to confirm their situation with Xenia, this caught us off guard. This man had never attempted to contact us, despite having been provided all means of contact for the rescue. "Hear back" was a puzzling phrase. They were waging "emotional blackmail", an all-too-common method some disreputable people use to gain leverage against a rescue to get what they want. Trespassing the love and the need to protect God's animals we are called to, they seek to coerce the outcome in their own favor. This was bad enough, but by attaching the time limit in a moment of false bravado, he had crossed the line of what was decent.

Apparently, he'd missed two crucial points: First, we would gladly have taken her back immediately if he'd simply said it wasn't working out. Our concern is for the kitten. Second, all our cats/kittens are microchipped for identification purposes. If she'd landed at the county shelter, we'd have been notified and could've picked her up there, knowing who had breached his adoption contract and abandoned her there.

I wasted no time, called the man, and headed right over to pick her up, emphasizing for him to keep her there until I arrived. My approach to reclaiming Xenia this time was doing what was necessary to secure her freedom from him; this would not be as pleasant an encounter as with the lady who'd found Xenia. This was a situation when hard lines needed to be drawn.

We arrived at the home to find glaring differences between what had been portrayed about the environment and what Xenia had been subject to these past couple months. The house was much smaller than represented, and we were greeted by the den of several boisterous dogs. There were three large breed dogs secured behind a gate in the kitchen area, breeds which are not known to be cat friendly. This house was much too small for the number of dogs, let alone a cat expected to survive here.

Immediately, I requested they bring Xenia out, along with her vetting records, given to them at the time of adoption. The little girl went into her room to pull Xenia out from under her bed, where we were told she'd been living in fear of the dogs during her time here. They seemed to think this was acceptable, remarking she wouldn't come out, as if they were puzzled. I was astounded. What happened when I followed up with them and was told everything was going great?

The little girl who had been so excited to adopt her brought Xenia out to me in some odd makeshift nylon cube, including the three toys I'd sent with her initially. (A genuine sign of how little attention or care she'd received under this roof.)

I settled her into the carrier we'd brought and could see the anxiousness in her face. After a few moments, she recognized my voice and seemed better. Gregg took her and set her near him while I finalized the business of her return.

The man told us he was sorry it hadn't worked out, when I promptly cut him off and stated we needed to get her home and settled. (It was amazing that he was looking for me to tell him it was ok).

I informed him we'd refund him the adoption fee, as was our policy. In some pretense that he wanted to do the honorable thing, that ship had sailed, he offered that we keep it as it had been a couple months. I did my best to respond in a business tone and insisted it be refunded. I hastily wrote out the check to reimburse him, stating I didn't want any part of this situation to touch Xenia. I didn't want his money. Then, turning to leave, I reminded him of the contract he had signed stating she was to be returned to us, a legally binding contract he had signed and was liable for. Then we left.

We secured Xenia in her carrier and I sat in the back seat trying to calm her and assure her she was safe.

"I am so sorry, Xenia," I whispered to her through my tears.

"You're okay sweet girl, you're safe. We'll go back home, and you can rest."

So many emotions flooded my heart at once. I felt intensely that I had failed her. Anger and outrage that this had happened to Xenia; hadn't she been through enough? Guilt and shame for having put her in this situation. I'd had the power to say no. Had I missed something? Had I just wanted her happily ever after so severely, I'd downplayed something to which I should have given more importance? I'd had a few nagging doubts. Did I just ignore them to get her adopted? (But be doers of the word, and not hearers only, deceiving yourselves. James 1:22)

We returned to the Manor, a familiar and safe place for her to relax and heal in. It was evident that the self-confident, happy kitten that had left the Manor was not the kitten returning to it now. This kitten was anxious and afraid, unsure what lay ahead next. I prayed that whatever emotional damage she'd suffered, time and love would heal her. All I wanted was for our outgoing, carefree girl to come back.

I prayed for Xenia, that the nervousness and frightened attitude would fade, and Xenia would be her charming old self again. And I prayed for forgiveness for having released her into that situation.

Xenia moved around the Manor slowly, sniffing, and taking it all in. She seemed to pick up some speed as she began recognizing familiar sights and sounds. Slight enthusiasm returned when she encountered things she remembered, like the faded scents of her friends she'd grown up with here, or her favorite area, toy corner. With recognition, she jumped onto her favorite cat condo to peer out the window briefly, then bounced up onto the sleeping loft overhead.

I watched her react to the things around her and wondered if it felt strange to her to be back without her buddies. I hoped the familiar surroundings were a comfort to her.

My heart hurt for her, my little warrior girl who had blossomed into a beautiful kitten at Doodlebug Manor. We were earnest in our promise to find her a better future, and then let her down. More than that, being a dynamic personality, charging into everything new as an adventure, with an unending energy, I wanted that back for her.

I was angry and guilty that she'd experienced this. Why hadn't I listened to that tiny voice in my head (God) warning me that something might be off? Was I so distracted by the idea that her home had come that I had subconsciously overlooked some signs I should've been more attentive to? Had I missed something, or not attributed enough importance to it? Had I misjudged Xenia's reaction or not really looked closely enough?

Well, she was home now, and she could take her time to heal and be with us.

Knowing she was coming back to us, and not wanting her to be alone during our vacation, we'd agreed to take in two sibling kittens (Bianca and Beau.) She hadn't warmed up to the kittens, avoiding them at every opportunity over the next few days, hissing if they encountered one another. Keeping her distance, she spent time on the catio or in the loft. The kittens had one another and didn't seem to mind.

Our old Xenia would've befriended them, but for now she kept her distance.

Before leaving on vacation, we touched base with our trusted pet-sitter, telling her about the situation with Xenia. She sent us pictures and updates daily so we could monitor her adjustment. Xenia stayed up in the loft, or she would hide behind the cabinets in the Manor, but we continued to believe that time and the safety of the Manor would heal and restore her.

Xenia began to heal, re-emerging, and behaving more like her old self again. Bianca and Beau had been adopted together, and the newest Doodlebugs to join the group since Xenia's return felt the benefit of her natural habit of welcoming them in.

There was a slightly different element to her now. Perhaps her experience had changed her a bit, making her more cautious, or maybe she was older and had naturally outgrown some of the younger kitten ways. Still, she was content, and resumed her role as the light of the Manor.

As an animal rescuer, the animal's welfare is always foremost in your intentions. Often, you're faced with emotional blackmail and threats from others who think there is something they can gain from it. (Example: Someone threatening to do harm or abandon a pet when a rescue is unable to take them.)

Sometimes, God calls us to work amongst the unscrupulous behavior and intentions of some humans incapable of unconditional love. We are called to navigate the situation and the conditions they apply with firm tones, firm boundaries and occasionally no second chances for the human involved, in order to protect His animals who love unconditionally by nature.

In some cases, the other is also true. Some situations call for extra grace and empathy for the human involved (Example: people who cannot provide care for an animal but struggle to release it from their custody.)

For the rescuer, it is the application of empathy and kindness, balanced with boundaries and consequences. Don't vindicate your heart at the risk of revealing too much vulnerability, while drawing the lines of acceptability with firmness and strength when needed.

This can be hard for Christians, as we can sometimes feel that our Christian piety comes from our ability to remain joyful and kind. However, in rescue, one must do what is necessary to remove the animal from the threat and get them to safety.

Xenia faced two encounters where it was necessary to step in and do what was needed to remove her from danger. The original lady, who found Xenia and her siblings, who had thought enough to call rescue but didn't care enough to do anything to assist, was easy enough in her approach. Applying grace and appealing to a sense of empathy resulted in the desired outcome.

In the second encounter, Xenia was in the hands of an owner who thought nothing of waging emotional blackmail and threats to gain what he wanted. The initial outreach back to this person was courteous, but firm. It was necessary to draw the lines for this man. It called out his unnecessarily aggressive approach, while denying him the exoneration of his treatment of both Xenia and the rescue.

Despite the struggles, Xenia, our warrior princess, was back, and it would take someone extra special to win her heart and ours the next time. Only an extraordinary home would do for our girl, and it would be forever this time.

But more with Xenia later, as her story did not end here.

> Behold, I am sending you out as sheep in the midst of wolves, so wise as serpents and innocent as doves. Matthew 10:16

> As for you, always be sober-minded, endure suffering, do the work of an evangelist, fulfill your ministry. 2 Timothy 4:5

Milo

With Miles to Go

I have miles to go before I sleep —Robert Frost

Lava lamps, hot plates, alcohol, and boyfriends are the most common things snuck into college housing. The next common is pets. However, one night, concerned undergrad, Jess at Vanderbilt chose a different route. She called me.

Like most of the cats who come to us as strays, we'll never know the exact details of how he came to be on his own on the streets.

Jess text messaged me looking for assistance, stating she was doing what she could to look after the cat. He was losing patches of fur due to constant scratching. They were feeding him on the sly. The apartment manager wanted him gone.

Returning a call to her, I gathered some additional details about the stray and his current situation.

She described him as a young, male tabby, (already neutered) maybe a year or two old. He was friendly, and not at all shy of people. I could hear the concern in her voice; she really wanted to help this little guy. We worked our way through my follow-up questions: No, they couldn't bring him inside. No, they had no friends or family who could take him. No, they didn't know where he had come from, just that he was there daily. There were no identifying tags or collar.

Sending over a couple of pictures via her cell phone, they were a little fuzzy, but good enough to look at his current condition. His pictures showed a medium-frame, gray tabby who resembled a tuxedo, only instead of the solid black 'jacket' of the tuxedo, he had gray striped tabby markings in three tones. His chest was a field of dirty white fur peeking through like a ruffled shirt with matching white gloves on his front paws. He had the white muzzle that came to a point on the upper bridge of his nose, speckled with tan spots resembling freckles. Large almond eyes, a pink nose, and beautiful long whiskers complimented his perfectly shaped face. He was skinny with that unkempt appearance strays usually have, but he was a handsome fellow despite his disheveled appearance

All signs pointed to his having been someone's pet: loved and cared for at one time, then carelessly discarded to survive on his own. It's a common practice in apartment complexes, let alone on college campuses. Residents move out and put their cats outdoors, left to their own devices. That he was neutered already was a sure sign that he had been someone's pet.

The rescue was full. We couldn't take in another cat full time, but we had to help him. It wasn't ideal, but we would have him vetted and work on finding him a new home. In the meantime, Jess couldn't bring him inside, but she would continue to feed and watch out for him.

Cats who spend time outside are subjected to so many dangers and diseases that our first order of business was to arrange his initial vet visit for a checkup, vaccines, and testing. Without providing indoor protection for him, we'd take the vetting one step at a time. This way we could balance the vetting and the related costs, with the timing of getting him situated in a safe, indoor home. Jess agreed to provide transportation and take him for the initial visit. We arranged for the vet to call us with the initial testing results and recommended the course of treatment. Doodlebug Manor would authorize payment through the rescue over the phone for the clinic. Jess texted me when they arrived at the vet's office with Willie and we all waited impatiently to hear the prognosis. It always feels like a lifetime to wait since so much is riding on the state of their condition. These are the first words we wait to hear and hope they turn out to be negative results. Some diagnoses can determine the course of action and what can be done for the cat, so we pray for the best.

When the phone rang, Jess was standing at the vet's office calling back with the results: Willie was FIV+.

My heart sank a little at the news, but while he tested positive for the virus, he showed no signs of it presenting. (Many times, with strays, preventative vaccines they may have had previously will show a positive result for the FIV and FELl virus present in the system, when it may really be residual serum showing up. It's highly recommended to have the test at least twice for an initial positive, to determine which it is.) The fact was that his diagnosis of FIV would present a more considerable challenge at finding an indoor home for him quickly. Time was our biggest challenge; the longer he remained outdoors, the longer he stayed at risk. Tragically, it was very likely that he contracted FIV while trying to survive on his own. The other scenario is that he was discarded to the streets if/when his former people discovered his diagnosis and were afraid of it or unwilling to provide care.

The rest of Willie's prognosis wasn't promising either. It turned out the hair loss was due to a flea allergy. Treatable but difficult for an outdoor cat to manage and survive. He had an infection from all the scratching and irritation which required steroids to help him heal, and would require regular medication for flea control to keep him healthy. With no identified indoor home to go to, the exposure to the outside elements and a lack of ongoing care could prevent him from healing or potentially bring about his end. Even a temporary safe, indoor placement would allow him to rest and heal, and afford some more time to find a permanent, loving home. Knowing his prognosis had just increased the urgency of finding him an indoor home.

I arranged payment for Willie's treatments, and he headed back with Jess where at least we knew he would be fed and watched over. All we could do was hope for the best and pray God's protection over him during the time it took to bring him inside. He had survived this long; he just needed to hang on a little longer. (God is our refuge and strength, a very present help in trouble. Psalm 46:1)

I began the campaign to find the right home to take Willie in via a large-scale search. Reaching out to my rescue contacts, especially those who worked with or took in FIV cats, veterinarians, and FIV+ dedicated groups through the internet. I reached specialized rescues, sanctuaries, and any other leads offered during the outreach. Rescuers reached out to other rescuers, and the word was out for him, only to come up empty.

Each day that passed while he remained outdoors was heartbreaking. His exposure to grass and fleas, the lack of protection when it rained, predators outside, all these elements resulted in the knowledge that each day could be his last. After what seemed like forever, the campaign to find a forever home had reached the right person.

A dear colleague and fellow cat lover, Katherine, who had adopted a couple of FIV+ cats from us a few years back, (Brewster & Lawson) had seen Willie's information via our social media campaign. She had read his story, seen his pictures, fallen in love with him, and wanted to welcome him into her home. Katherine was a cat lover with specialized experience working with and caring for FIV cats, and she had a soft spot for them in her heart. He didn't know it yet, but he had hit the jackpot.

Katherine had relocated out of state a few years back, so I began making the arrangements with a professional transport group to take Milo, his new name, to go with his new home, a good 14 hours away.

Once the transport details were set, we arranged for Milo to join us at Doodlebug Manor for a couple nights so he could settle in and rest before his long trip. A couple of nights of knowing he was safe, comfortable in the air conditioning, and having a full tummy would do wonders for him.

I reached out to Jess immediately to let her know he had found a fantastic home and his transport arrangements were made; he'd be leaving in two days, now all we needed was Milo!

She agreed to bring him to us at the Manor. He looked good when she arrived with Milo. The infections were mostly cleared up, and he looked less disheveled. The anti-itch medicine had helped him recover. Now he would have the home and meds he needed to stay healthy.

We are always cautious when introducing an adult cat into the Doodlebug community, so we set up a comfortable area for him inside our usual dog crate decked out with comforts and food. Milo was exhausted from his struggle to survive outside alone, and so he snuggled into soft blankets, content to feel safe, and slept.

Our efforts to introduce him to the gang at Doodlebug Manor the following day went exceptionally well. Within the first few minutes, he had charmed everyone, human and feline alike, with such a sweet temperament. Milo was gentile, well mannered, and purred from the moment I sat down to get to know him. He was curious about the cats and kittens coming by to greet him, but mostly he liked to have his head stroked and relax in the blankets. This was one sweet cat, and his accessible introduction into our group was a great indicator he would do just as well in his new home.

The day arrived when it was time for him to begin the journey to his new home. I packed his suitcase (items he would need both for the trip and to have some things to call his own in his new home) and settled him into a new comfy travel cage. One last check and off we went.

Tucked inside his suitcase was the most excellent note from Jess addressed to his new 'mom,' which shared some details of the first part of Milo's story; how they had found him and already come to love him. It went on to thank Katherine for saving his future and giving him a loving home.

Reaching the parking lot where we'd agreed to meet, I stretched my legs and checked on Milo in the back of my car. This is where the transport team would meet us and take Milo for the next leg of his journey. The transport family arrived, welcoming Milo and settling him in for the long journey in the comfortable back of their SUV.

Telling Milo to be on his best behavior for the journey and to rest, I told him it had been my distinct pleasure knowing him. I assured him he was heading off to a dream home. I knew Katherine, and he was off to the best kind of home; he'd be secure and happy from here on out. It was a tearful goodbye, but joyful, too.

Milo hadn't stayed with us long, but the impact of caring for and knowing him was profound. It was an honor to be a part of his story. Knowing he was on his way to the loving home he so craved and deserved made my heart light. I watched as the SUV pulled out with Milo, taking him on to the next chapter in his story. This would be the last leg of a long struggle for him, and at the end, he would finally arrive at his happily ever after.

Watching them go from the parking lot, I offered a prayer that God would watch over him and see him safely to his new beginning, and then I headed home. (The Lord will keep you from all evil; he will keep your life. The Lord will keep your going out and your coming in from this time forth and forevermore. Psalm 121:7–8)

Katherine kept us informed of Milo's arrival, sending periodic updates on how he was adapting in his new home. He had been exhausted on arrival, but was happy and blending into his new environment effortlessly. He enjoyed her other cats and had found a special buddy, Connor. Milo indeed found his happily ever after.

Not long ago, Jess contacted us to inquire after him, wanting to know how he was doing now, a few years later. We shared some pictures with her that Katherine had recently sent, noting he was now a solid 12.6 lbs, loving life as an indoor kitty. The people in Milo's circle who love him are connected, just reminding us how profoundly the lives we touch affect our own.

When things were looking the worst for Milo, the help we tried to bring was stagnant. Despite our best efforts, we could not provide for his needs, only try to sustain him. When the days dragged, leaving him exposed to the elements, we feared all was for naught. God answered our prayers, stepping in and bringing the way for Milo. (And my God will supply every need of yours according to his riches in glory in Christ Jesus. Philippians 4:19 ESV)

God would not have taken us on this journey and left us alone. I wish I had held on to this promise from God sooner, living with the peace and knowledge that God would provide for Milo.

...for he has said, “I will never leave you nor forsake you” Hebrews 13:5

I have said these things to you, that in Me you may have peace. In the world you have tribulation. But take heart; I have overcome the world. John 16:33

Lucy II

Going Home

"Home is where your story begins" —Annie Danielson

"Rumor has it they're closing by the end of next month. They lost their lease and have 30 days to vacate the property! So much for a long-term sanctuary."

The statement came from a rescue acquaintance sitting at the opposite end of the table. Several local rescuers had settled together for the lunch break during a meeting of the local PSI chapter. (Pet Sitters International[5])

Following my involuntary intake of breath in response, I slowly exhaled despite the feeling that I'd been sucker punched. An all-consuming mix of dread, sadness, and fear hit me. Pushing through this initial onslaught of feelings, I asked the question I didn't want the answer to, anyway: "*What about the animals in their care? What are they doing about them?*" I asked.

This was the sanctuary we'd placed Lucy with just shy of a year ago! She was undergoing healing and stabilization, and was settled and happy alongside her buddy George, the orange tabby. (See Lucy the Overcomer.) This was to have been her happily ever after and the girl had earned it! Lucy had traveled a hard road to get there, and we had walked alongside her just hoping to find the right place for her. Our last update from the sanctuary not long ago indicated all was well.

There were no answers to my question coming from this group. I needed the facts. I walked outside and called the couple who ran the sanctuary to get the full story. During that discussion, several things became clear: they had to close due to the loss of their lease. They'd been given 30 days with a small margin of leeway to place all the animals currently in their care, and they were unable to keep any of them. Yes, Lucy was still there along with George. Yes, they were the only two cats there needing to be rehomed. Yes, they would release them both to Doodlebug Manor so we could place the cats. They were working with a couple of dog rescues to see the dogs rehomed.

Exiting the meeting, I began planning the next steps for both cats during the drive home. We'd agreed they both would stay at the sanctuary farm for now with the hope their placement would happen before the 30 days. (This reduced the number of adjustments the cats would have to make.) If not, we would return to collect them both and continue their adoption efforts from there.

Losing the sanctuary was heartbreaking for the animals residing there and the proprietors who were also losing their dream. This was the first sanctuary of its kind in our area. A place that offered a peaceful farm setting and included not only indoor space but fenced outdoor acreage for the animals' comfort. Their premise was to take in pets in need and to provide rehab, rehoming, and long-term care for the animals that were older or no longer adoptable. Not only would those services disappear for the pets, but their care and placement fell to the already overburdened rescue community.

I offered a prayer asking God to watch over His animals and keep them safe. *"You are God's loving creatures. I pray that you are led to your right place quickly and safely."*

Disappointment and distress were at the forefront of this unexpected change. Lucy's placement here had seemed like a miracle. Now we faced an uncertain future for her again. The anxiety of losing another home and having to adjust to new circumstances was looming in her future. Added to that was the pressure of trying to place both cats before the 30 days expired. Beyond those 30 days, we would have the challenge of where to house both Lucy and George while we worked to place them.

We knew little about George's life prior to his placement at the sanctuary, but he was a beautiful cat, with the popular orange tabby temperament; friendly, easygoing, and affectionate. Losing a home is never easy for any animal, and he faced those same adjustments.

Pulling together the pictures and details of Lucy's past, I assembled her profile, preparing to share it and elicit assistance from our local rescuers. Most of them who knew me knew her story, including one fellow rescuer who had posted the gripping picture of Lucy I'd taken of her when she was down to two pounds sitting in that cage at the shelter. The story we told started with her struggle to survive the county shelter, to her recovery and placement, to the current loss of her most recent home. Adding in the information we gleaned on George from the sanctuary, and the pictures I'd taken of him the day Lucy had arrived there, we finished George's portfolio as well.

We posted both cats to our adoption site and via a huge social media campaign to reach as many potential adopters as possible. I prayed God would bring the right people for these sweet cats and guide us in our efforts. It felt like they'd deserved a happy ending but had been dealt a false start. Well, nothing was guaranteed in the world of rescue, we knew that. We held strong to the resolve we felt to find that coveted happy ending for both, and that God would provide the way.

Lucy and I had forged a bond of love and trust during her initial struggles, and as a rescue we were loyal to the commitment we'd made. "Once a Doodlebug, always a Doodlebug." George, through his association with Lucy and the fact that he was a wonderful cat, had won that loyalty as well. He was an honorary Doodlebug.

I prayed for God to guide me through the process and to give me the wisdom to follow His lead. (Commit your work to the Lord, and your plans will be established. Proverbs 16:3)

Not long after the word was out for both cats, our campaign yielded some results with a couple of promising applications coming in. We would be particularly choosy when selecting the new homes for both cats. Meanwhile, I'd begun contacting the sanctuary for the vet and healthcare records for both cats. Standardly, we provide those to all adopters. (Veterinarians would not release records to rescues without the express consent of the current or last owners they had on file and a signed release to do so. This made it important to send the request immediately to allow time to collect those records for the new adopters.)

Gregg and I were chatting with our friends and longtime supporters of the rescue, Marci and Rex (you've met them before in the story of Dusty), one afternoon. Sharing the latest Doodlebug Manor goings on, we told them what was happening with Lucy and George. They had lived through the original rescue events of Lucy's story along with us, and knew well all she'd been through. They immediately wanted to take Lucy in and give her the forever home she so longed for. They were called to welcome her into their pack and provide the love and stability she needed. Lucy had hit the jackpot this time. This would be her home at last. Our hearts felt light and thankful for this wonderful turn of events.

That left George. The inquiries about him had been coming in and we'd identified a couple of strong candidates among them. We picked a wonderful family with younger children to become George's adoptive family. They were seeking so many of the characteristics in their next pet, which George embodied, that they seemed a well-suited match. They are experienced cat owners and were extremely excited when we reached back out to them. This family welcomed George in and gave him his place to belong. Knowing he was truly wanted and on his way home made us smile. I offered a quick prayer that this time was forever.

We made arrangements for Lucy and George to join their new families, and though they weren't together now, their friendship had sustained them through their time at the sanctuary, making their shared environment their home for a time.

Over the next couple months, as some details emerged within the community around the final closing of the sanctuary, some speculation arose around how the conditions there had deteriorated.

Perhaps things were not quite as they'd been portrayed. Whether or not all these tales were true, we'll never know. We wouldn't have given it much credence until an odd set of circumstances around Lucy came to light for us.

Lucy's family had reached out to request the complete set of records from her former vet when they noticed a rather apparent scar on her ear, and a gap in her routine care from the original records the sanctuary had provided. Since we had requested the complete records from the sanctuary for both cats, but they omitted pages from what we'd been provided, it opened room for questions. Reaching back to the sanctuary to mention the gap of care in the records, we inquired about the scar, only to be told they knew nothing about it. We knew Lucy hadn't had a scar before her arrival there.

The vet records indicated that Lucy had undergone wound care during her time with the sanctuary listing the cause of injury as a dog attack. In light of the omitted records and their dishonesty around the attack she suffered, we speculated about the true conditions that may have existed there for the animals. Knowing things might not have been what we thought eased our initial sadness around needing to rehome them. It was a relief to know that all the animals who had formerly lived there had been successfully rehomed.

God could see far past what we could, and knowing things were not as they should've been for Lucy and George, He called us to right the circumstances for them both. (But the LORD said to Samuel "do not look on his appearance or on the height of his stature, because I have rejected him. For the LORD sees not as man sees: man looks on the outward appearance, but the LORD looks on the heart" 1 Samuel 16:7)

George's family reached out to us shortly after his adoption to let us know he was doing well, and it thrilled them to have him. We were happy to know he had a complete family to belong to and was truly wanted. He was a great cat, and it was heartwarming to know he was where he was appreciated and loved.

The controversy and struggles Lucy had endured in her young life behind her, she was content to set them aside and settle into her new life in her new home. Lucy merged quickly into her new crew of cat peeps. She was entertaining as, one by one, her individual quirks emerged, and her true persona emerged. Lucy tended to 'mother' the other cats, whether they welcomed this or not! Putting the cats in a headlock and grooming them was her way of nurturing her new family. Lucy, petite in stature and giving the impression she is fragile and tiny, developed a special bond with their cat Rocky. (You'll meet Rocky in an upcoming chapter). Her favorite game is to ambush him, taking him by surprise, and enticing him into wrestling matches. She loves to play and finds any excuse to jump up in the air as high as she can, forming an arc, like a rainbow, and then descends slowly, gracefully like a dancer. Despite the hardships and anguish she survived on her journey, Lucy overcame it and is a happy girl in her forever home.

In rescue, our mission is to save all the souls God sends our way. This is our covenant, so we follow God's lead when He calls us to service. We can't always foresee when the need arises to save them again. For what may be beyond the reach of our sight is clear and present for God. Sometimes, once we clock-out thinking we've met the needs of the animals, God beckons us to clock back into a pet's life. We are honored to be chosen again to be in service to God and His animals.

We are so glad that God pulled us back into Lucy's story, not only to ensure her happiness, but to have the blessing of knowing it for sure. We are twice blessed to have gained the connection to George. Without Lucy's relationship with him, we would not have been able to save him. And as always, we know God loves His animals and will provide for them always. While they may be beyond our reach, they are never beyond His.

It's a blessing to be called into God's army to protect and rescue these precious souls.

> And let us not grow weary of doing good, for in due season we will reap, if we do not give up. Galatians 6:9

> Now faith is the assurance of things hoped for, the conviction of things not seen. For by it the people of old received their commendation. By faith we understand that the universe was created by the word of God, so that what is

seen was not made out of things that are visible. Hebrews 11:1–3

Vinnie

The Love Bug

Holding on is believing there's only a past; letting go is knowing that there's a future —Daphne Rose Kingma

The day the matching kittens arrived, we were impressed by their appearance and demeanor. Two kittens discovered perched on the lower branches of a tree arching over the main walking trail in a popular area park had just arrived. They were rescued by the same family who discovered them, a lady and her two children. They brought them to us at the suggestion of a mutual friend.

No one could say for sure, but the most likely story is that someone had dumped them in the park, due to their healthy, well-nourished appearance. Chances were they weren't outdoors on their own for long and may've been soliciting help by going where the people were. They were so similar in appearance and age that they may have been siblings, but were at least former housemates trying to survive together.

Both kittens were 14–16 weeks old, short-haired orange tabbies, one male, one female. (It's unusual to find a female orange tabby, most are male.) We named the male Vinnie. He was a deep orange, with stripes of an even deeper amber tone, the same stripes forming decorative rings on the last half of his long tail. His head was triangular with a longer muzzle, a pink nose tip, and beautiful, long white whiskers. His eyes matched his beautiful amber hue, giving him a sleek look. He had an easy, content character right from the start. We called the female Buttercup after the wildflowers in the fields and parks. She was a lighter, champagne orange with a heart-shaped face that was a little rounder with white accents lining her golden eyes and highlighting her cheeks and lower lip. The effect was an almost 'kissable' look. She had the same sleek one-tone continuity, with fur texture that was just a little fluffier.

Our two newest Doodlebugs were a little older than most of the community of younger kittens in the Manor, but were still young enough to blend in perfectly. They both settled in contentedly from the start. Buttercup was friendly and quiet, a little reserved at first, preferring to observe the activity around her before jumping into anything. It didn't take long until she felt safe enough to be a part of the gang. Yet she always remained a little shyer than Vinnie, who didn't really know the meaning of the word shy. He was outgoing and vivacious, just the friendly 'cat next door.' He bounced from one new playmate to another, making the Manor his own.

He instantly charmed the other kittens, tackling, playing, and grooming. Vinnie had just stepped right into the role of big brother. Many kittens had come in 'solo' rather than part of a litter. This set Vinnie up as a role model, a protector of sorts; and together they created a family structure for them all to belong to.

It had transpired so easily and naturally that we knew it was meant to be.

This season turned out to be one of my favorites in rescue. (And all these blessings shall come upon you and overtake you, if you obey the voice of the LORD your God. Deuteronomy 28:2)

Throughout the coming weeks and months, the rescue continued to thrive, with many of the kittens adopted and new ones taking their place at the Manor. Buttercup was adopted and off to her new home, while Vinnie continued welcoming the newcomers and looked after them all. It seemed he'd found his niche as a 'Big Brother.'

He was content in his world, yet it had weighed on me that Vinnie's home hadn't found him yet. He was growing into a very handsome, charming young man. It would be a challenge for anyone not to adore him.

We know that in rescue you never really know which cats will be adopted when it depends on when their intended families find them, but with his charming persona we really expected Vinnie would be adopted quickly. At the same time, I knew Vinnie was an extraordinary soul, and that God must have chosen an extraordinary home for him. They were on their way, in their time.

We loved Vinnie as part of the family, and he would be welcome to stay forever if left up to our hearts, but that wasn't the life I wanted for him. He continually gave so much to so many others, many of whom had blossomed under his care and found their own homes. We wanted that happy ending for Vinnie. But for now, Vinnie had the love and admiration of many!

As one season turned into the next, we continued to be aware that he still had not found his permanent home. Where was his special person, and what was taking them so long to find him?

Summer had arrived, evidenced by the cats gravitating to warm window ledges to nap, or directly underneath the sky lights. The catio attached to the rescue resembled drive-time traffic with the crowds of kitties making their way out to lie in the sun, lazily bat at a bug or butterfly that happened by, or stare into the surrounding garden and catch a whiff of catnip. It was the hot spot during the warm months, in more ways than one!

Surrounded by kittens, my only adult boy was so companionable that I gave him a few liberties. He was allowed to come out into the yard with me to play in the sun while I gardened or sat in a lawn chair. He would chase this or dash at that, and true to Vinnie's persona, he became fast friends with our Sheltie-mix dog, Rikki. The two of them would chase all around our backyard, doing laps around the pool, back and forth along the length of the fence, and eventually collapse side by side to rest under the shade trees.

Vinnie had been posted on our adoptable cat's webpage for some time now, with no inquiries. It was baffling to me. Although we know that God's timing is always perfect, it is difficult to be patient when we cannot see it! We'd updated his profile periodically to keep things interesting and share the uniqueness of him. We captured adorable pictures of Vinnie and posted them. (My favorite is the candid shot of him casually draped across the velvety, red child size recliner in the Manor. He so owned that moment, like a king on his throne!)

Finally, after so long, we decided to leave his profile up through the end of the week. If we hadn't had any inquiries by then, we'd remove his profile for a while. Once the market of current adopters has seen a cat in their searches over time, it's better to pull the profile, wait a few weeks or more, then relist the cat to find a new group of potential adopters. Similar to real estate listings, a posting that stays up too long can cause speculation about 'why.' Is there something wrong with the cat?

If that time came, we would consider keeping him. We loved him, and he fit right in with our family. Maybe this was meant to be?

We couldn't help but feel in our hearts that this special boy was meant as someone's beloved cat. We had a good number of pets at the time, and my desire for Vinnie was to have a home where he would receive a lot of special attention and love without the competition of so many other cats. But for now, he was content and loved his life, so he would remain with us. We knew whoever adopted Vinnie would have to appreciate what a unique and special boy he was.

Friday morning came and by midafternoon, still no inquiries had come in.

With a sad heart, I removed Vinnie's profile. Vinnie was content and knew he was loved, so maybe that's what he wanted. I offered a prayer that whatever was meant to be for this sweet boy would be, and that I would recognize it. (For everything there is a season, and a time for every matter under heaven; Ecclesiastes 3:1)

A quiet peace about Vinnie filled my heart as I finished my prayer.

Just minutes later, a Facebook message popped up with an inquiry about him. (God's timing!)

A potential adopter was asking if he was still available to meet or had he been adopted? There was an element of anxiousness in the inquiry, and my heart leapt a little. The lady explained that she and her husband had lost their beloved orange tabby and had been watching the posts about Vinnie. They hadn't responded right away as they were mourning and wanted to be sure they were ready to adopt again.

They really wanted to meet him and had decided it was time when his profile had disappeared! She hoped it didn't mean he'd been adopted; they'd contacted me immediately.

"I'm so glad you contacted me," I shared. "I just removed his information minutes ago. No, he's not adopted. We were just giving him some time off the adoption pages."

"We've been watching his profile and feel like we are ready to meet him!" she responded. "Would this afternoon be too soon? We can come right over."

"Today would be fine," I replied. "Let me give you the address."

And just like that, Vinnie had his first suitors. I knew they would fall in love upon meeting him, so we chatted for a few moments before they arrived. Reassuring Vinnie that the decision on whether these were his people was his. And even so, we would be here for him if he was ever in need.

Vinnie was adopted and went home with the couple who'd reached out that day. He waited and his family arrived to get him. His new home offered a house equipped with everything a cat would love, including two new brother cats. Vinnie was settled now in a comfortable home with two people who were excited to have him. Additionally, he had a wonderful, enclosed porch room complete with beautiful huge windows overlooking the landscaping outside, not so different from the catio he loved at the Manor.

God had already chosen the perfect home for Vinnie—he was allowing them the time they needed to heal and be ready to adopt again, when they could dedicate their hearts to a new cat. God's timing was perfect for Vinnie and his adopters, bringing blessings and love into their lives. We could never have known the reason for God's timing, but it was beautiful.

The years have brought wonderful opportunities to continue to visit with Vinnie. I always look forward to his shared stories and pictures in his wonderful home life. God graced me with a bonus blessing, knowing how much I loved him. Vinnie's new parents live close by, and we still visit Vinnie to this day.

When I asked them later, what had prompted them to reach out that afternoon when they contacted me? What had drawn them to Vinnie? They shared they felt they'd gotten to know him by watching his story on the adoption site; they felt they'd been watching him grow up all along.

But the final thing they fell in love with was the cavalier pose in the picture of him draped across the plush red recliner and the look in his eye. There is a twinkle that is uniquely Vinnie, and they recognized it.

God puts the same need to love and protect one another on the hearts of His animals just as he does His people. He has blessed Vinnie with a loving, nurturing heart and a wonderful sense of contentment wherever he goes.

Just as God tells Christians to put our trust in Him and know that we are loved and protected, the same love is extended to His animals. (The Lord is my rock and my fortress and my deliverer, my God, my rock, in whom I take refuge, my shield, and the horn of my salvation, my stronghold. Psalm 18:2)

Some of the anxiety I'd felt around Vinnie's adoption date was due to my dread over the impending goodbye it would bring. (A 'rip the band aid off' reflex.) I loved Vinnie and wanted that special home for him, but wanted to hang on to our special bond, too. While I accepted that the adoption would come in God's time, He blessed us even more by arranging a continued relationship with this special cat, in addition to the right home.

Now, when I reminisce about Vinnie's story, there is a lesson God had for me even then, which I see more clearly now; there is no need to own those you love. Love is a universally binding blessing, one of the few things that expands and grows in our lives the more we give away. We can love freely, and without strings, as love is a real, everlasting thing that can even transcend death, as Christ's love for us has done!

Beloved, let us love one another, for love is from God, and whoever loves has been born of God and knows God. I John 4: 7

And above all these put on love, which binds everything together in perfect harmony. Colossians 3:14

Rocky

The Cat Next Door

How we behave toward cats here below determines our status in heaven. —Robert A. Heinlein

We pulled into the driveway just in time to witness our neighbor Angie step out into her garage and begin to dance and scream. Looking around her feet frantically, just as something small and black darted from the garage into the front shrubs between our houses.

“What is it?! What is that?!” she shouted while throwing an empty plastic milk jug at the tiny creature in a state of near panic.

It was difficult to tell from the green eyes looking out at us from behind the hedgerow. We could make out jet black fur and a hunched-down posture from where we stood. We had an inkling this was nothing to fear.

Gregg and I both sprang into rescue action. He moved in closer to see the creature to confirm, while I grabbed the Kevlar gloves from the cat emergency kit in the back of my car.

"It's okay," Gregg confirmed. "It's a cat."

Angie's anxiety disappeared instantly, and she returned to us with a bowl of milk for the cat.

Still unsure what we were dealing with here (an aggressive, or scared cat), Gregg set up the large dog cage in our open garage and I tucked a blanket inside. Gregg was prepared to flush the cat out while I moved into position to grab him. He reached over, prepared to scruff him if needed to pull him out, but the minute he picked him up, the little black waif went semi-limp, and all 'ran to the bottom.' (A term used for how a cat's weight shifts down when picked up, feeling like they are sliding through your hands like a sack of sand.)

"I think we'll be okay," Gregg commented, half teasing, as he handed him to me to place in the cage.

This little black cat had huge, rounded auburn eyes, a broad forehead, and a friendly face. About a quarter of his tongue stuck out between his lips in a relaxed state and he looked at us with a curious but not particularly frightened expression. He was small and in rough shape. Runny eyes, visible bite wounds on his torso and legs and a plug of fur missing on the side of his neck. No open bleeding or gashes, thank goodness. Especially given it was a Sunday morning, so our usual vet's office was closed. Nothing seemed emergent, so we outfitted his cage to make him comfortable, added food and water, and covered the cage with a sheet two thirds of the way so he could relax and settle. (Not that he seemed the least bit rattled.)

We moved him into the extra bedroom that afternoon as a quarantine and healing space set up for our new guest to be comfortable and where he would be easy to care for. We covered a cage under the window so he could choose to sit on top (Dog crates have a hatched metal top, hard to sit on without something laid across them.) and look out the window. His litter was pushed in the back for privacy, and his food dishes were just outside the front of the cage. He had a full run of the room and a queen size guest bed to rest on facing the television, which ran a constant stream of videos for cats. We included some toys for him to try out while he healed. We named our little survivor "Rocky" after whatever he'd endured but survived outside on his own.

Rocky was fighting a solid URI (Upper Respiratory Infection). A few bite wounds and scratches from some skirmish he'd encountered covered his lower end and abdomen, and there was an odd hole in the side of his neck. It was hard to really tell what was going on there as it was scarred over with all the fur missing. By all indications, it was most likely a wolf worm that had burrowed into his neck but was now long gone. (Also called cuterebra or warbles, they are parasites that cause a lot of pain and infection in cats. They're relatively common and need treatment right away. When identified, the warble will be removed, and the injured tissues will be surgically removed. Antibiotics are usually prescribed to combat any secondary bacterial infection.)

Following his vet visit the next day and a stream of medications, he spent his first few nights with us eating as much as he could, resting and looking out the window. We'd leave the window slightly open at the bottom to let in the fresh air for him, and he curled up on the windowsill, staring out. I wasn't sure what he was missing out there, perhaps just the freedom of roaming as he pleased, but I wondered what he was longing for. It didn't appear the outdoor life had been that kind to him.

He was healing nicely and improving each day. He seemed to like our company, though we struggled to understand what to do to entertain him as he recovered. Rocky's past was a mystery. He was a young adult, certainly not feral, but no signs indicated he'd been someone's cat either. There was no microchip to identify him, and he hadn't been neutered yet. There were no collar or tags, no way to know if he'd ever had any vaccines, and he seemed more baffled by the toys in his room than interested in them. All the things we would generally look at for clues to his past weren't painting a clear picture. What was certain was that he was a sweet-natured boy and wouldn't have lasted much longer on his own outside.

A few weeks after his final vetting and healing time, Rocky had adjusted to life as an indoor cat and was doing wonderfully. He was proving to be a mellow, charming young man with a penchant for catnip. It seemed the time had come to introduce Rocky to the rest of the Doodlebugs in the rescue, allowing him to cohabitate with other cats, and enjoy all the perks of living in the Manor.

Rocky's full charm came to light in the Manor, he was an instant hit with the other cats, adults and kittens alike. Without really seeking it, Rocky had become the popular guy, the one everyone wanted to hang out with. Rocky did well with the attention of the others, but still preferred his alone time as well.

Rocky had shown up in need not long after we'd lost our own 'mellow' cat, Baxter, at 12 years old. He'd been one of the cats from our feral clan behind the house we had worked for TNR, though Baxter was never feral. He, too, had arrived as a gentle soul and was popular with the other cats. We'd suddenly lost Baxter after a short illness and still missed him terribly. Though these two boys looked nothing alike, (Baxter had been a champagne orange tabby, stockier in build with a rounder face), their similarities reminded us of one another.

Although it wasn't uncommon for cats to show up in the neighborhood needing assistance as Rocky had, we had often thought 'the word was out' about us among the cats in the neighborhood, or an invisible 'welcome cats' sign hung on our door. After all, even years before we'd first moved to the house, the feral colony behind the house awaited us.

In this case, Gregg and I are convinced that Baxter reached out to guide Rocky to our door. (Although Rocky had missed us by one driveway, he'd found his way.) Even during his time with us on Earth, Baxter had always been a nurturing soul among our group, looking out for the younger or smaller cats. Through the years, we've witnessed the love and compassion that goes on between animals, during the normal course of things, and particularly in times of illness or death. Their mode of communication is at a much more spiritual level, with each other and humans. This was just the type of thing Baxter would do.

One afternoon during a get together with friends, Marcie & Rex, (also cat-lovers we've met before in the stories of Dusty and Lucy) we were sharing the loss of Baxter and the appearance of Rocky just a few days later. They had seen the pictures of Rocky we'd posted on social media and the background of his story and wanted to meet him. They had known Baxter well and agreed that God had sent Baxter to show Rocky the way to our house. That just seemed right. They adored the description of his little tongue that always stuck out, and how he had shown up in need.

Rocky went with them to begin life in his new forever home. He has grown into a big cat, fully filled-out and healthy. No surprise to us, he is the popular guy in their cat group, and particularly close to Lucy. Choosing to curl up on Rex nightly for a cuddle before bed, we look forward to the stories and the pictures we are blessed to share with our friends. Rocky is one of a kind, and we are delighted to hear about his continuing antics and the joy he brings to their home.

God knew we were there to help and that Rocky needed assistance. We have no doubt that the timing of our meeting, the fact that it was unavoidable in our neighbor's driveway and the proximity to our loss of Baxter, that it was part of God's plan to find the help for Rocky that he needed and help us heal over losing Baxter. Helping Rocky helped ease our sorrow and pain and the feeling of helplessness around the loss of Baxter. It also increased our soul family with the addition of Rocky.

Sometimes as Christians, we are timid about recognizing and celebrating the spiritual wonders that God sends our way. Animals are a gift of unconditional love, friendship, and sometimes mentors to guide us through our journey on Earth. They are our spiritual brothers and sisters, and we rejoice in those spiritual connections.

> Then shall your light break forth like the dawn, and your healing shall spring up speedily... Isaiah 58:8
>
> Let each of us please his neighbor for his good, to build him up. Romans 15:2
>
> Whoever is righteous has regard for the life of his beast, but the mercy of the wicked is cruel. Proverbs 12:10
>
> God is our refuge and strength, a very present help in trouble. Psalm 46:1 ESV

Xenia II

Finally Home

Life takes you to unexpected places. Love brings you home. —Melissa McClone

"Oh Mel, I am so sorry," I choked out, trying to maintain my composure enough to speak.

"He was such a great cat. I can't believe he's gone. Ferrell is lost without him." Ferrell had been Mick's choice and had formed a special bond with him. (See Mick and Zeke.)

They'd had to say goodbye to Mick today, after only 6 short years with him. His departure followed a valiant fight against cancer, and it was too soon to say goodbye. Offering words of comfort and love, I tried to console my friend as we cried together. She reminisced about the day they'd adopted Mick and Zeke together, remarking on how naturally they fit into their home. (*Had it really been 6 years ago?)*

As she spoke, fond memories and images of Mick and the story of his life with us played through my mind, beginning with his arrival at Doodlebug Manor and the day he'd chosen them to be his family, along with his brother Zeke.

As our conversation ended, Mel added, "Well, we are grateful we had him for these last 6 years."

My mind kept returning to Mick that evening as I spent time with the current rescue cats. Reminiscing about his favorite spot to sleep, and how he would hang out in the loft under the skylight. I shared these memories out loud with the cats. None of them would have known Mick from direct contact, but perhaps they knew his energy and scent from within the walls of the Manor. The stories of former Doodlebugs and their happily ever afters remained legendary to the current Doodlebugs. The power of those successful adoptions was a part of the Manor that surrounded them daily. I like to think that picking up on the positive energy and hearing stories of the cats that had gone before them gives them hope as they await their forever homes.

Tonight, they would recognize my energy levels being 'off' due to mourning, so I shared with them the reason for my sadness in losing Mick.

Xenia was the first one to notice my demeanor. She knew me best of all the current Doodlebugs. We had experienced some of these same emotions together because of her failed first adoption. She was back here with us to heal and catch her breath. She was doing beautifully again, playful, content, and regaining her confidence. Falling into step with me, she was offering me her companionship.

It seemed right that she would be the one to share the story of Mick with, as I had shared the story of her adoption trauma with Melissa and Ferrell when it happened. They had reacted as outraged as I'd felt and had followed her recovery. They were also great supporters of the rescue, and Melissa would come for 'play dates' with the kittens to help socialize them, earning her the nickname 'Aunt Mel.'

Doodlebug continued over the next few weeks as usual with kittens finding their wonderful homes, and new kittens joining us for their chance at the same. We are always careful and selective in choosing the adopters for our kittens. When it came to Xenia, I was extremely protective. I didn't list her on our adoption pages, not yet. We were in no hurry, and knew it would have to be an outstanding, out of the ordinary home to even be considered.

Xenia had already beaten the odds twice in her young life; surviving abandonment outdoors at a very young age along with the loss of her littermates, and then later through the fiasco that was her first adoption through no fault of her own. (See Xenia The Patient Warrior) Any potential adopter would have a meaningful appreciation of this little warrior. The key would recognize her enormous heart and her special zest for life.

She was back with us now, in what she identified as home, and in no hurry to trust again. When potential adopters would visit the Manor, Xenia would quietly disappear into the loft. She would stay out of sight until the unfamiliar voices, strange noises, and scents dissipated. When the normal ambience returned, so would Xenia.

We'd been praying steadily for her. Praying that she would overcome any residual pain or anxiety from her misadventure and that her heart would heal again. Around those she knew, she was comfortable and calm. She just needed time for God to heal her fully. (For everyone who has been born of God overcomes the world. And this is the victory that has overcome the world—our faith. John 5:4)

Considering what she'd endured, I wondered if it might not be such a bad thing to have a little 'stranger danger' in her soul, to protect her future.

One afternoon, glancing down at my cell phone, I saw an incoming call from Mel. She mentioned how lost and lonely Zeke was without his buddy Mick. (Zeke had decided early on that the two of them were bonded and adored his big brother.) He was forlorn and didn't know quite what to do with himself. They had decided he needed a companion, and they were all ready, so they'd like to come visit with the Doodlebugs to find the right kitten.

This was music to my ears. These were excellent cat parents we wished would adopt all our rescue kitties. We were elated that one of our kittens would land a fantastic home with them. We were looking forward to the visit.

A couple of evenings before the visit, Ferrell had called. He mentioned they'd been talking about what age and gender of kitten would be the best companion for Zeke. They'd decided they had their hearts set on seeing if Xenia would be that kitten. They felt she'd be an excellent fit if I agreed. Of course, they would want to become reacquainted with her during their visit to ensure things went well. We all decided it was important for Xenia to meet them and make her decision. They felt she would be a fantastic sister for Zeke, and he would also be a blessing to her. They wanted to give her a loving home, guaranteeing her a happy life.

I prayed after that call for the guidance and knowledge to make the right decision this time for Xenia. And mostly I prayed she would choose this home to be hers, as I already knew she'd be well cared for and loved. (May the God of hope fill you with all joy and peace in believing, so that by the power of the Holy Spirit you may abound in hope. Romans 15:13)

The evening they arrived, the Manor exploded with excitement. The kittens ran in all directions, playing and vying for their attention. Something new and different was always exciting for the cats.

As we settled in for their visit, we chatted around how Zeke was doing, and the excitement of bringing a new cat into the home. As we spoke, I noticed from the corner of my eye that Xenia was showing an interest in our visitors, rather than making her usual hasty retreat to the loft. Whether she recognized Mel's voice from her visits to the Manor, or sensed the energy of these two cat lovers, her interest was piqued. She was cautious, observing from across the room, and taking her time with a slow, methodical approach. She slid behind the condo here, then, taking a few steps closer, ducked behind the toy chest while peeking out to see if she'd been spotted. I caught Mel's eye and darted my eyes toward where Xenia was making her interested approach.

Neither of us acknowledged her directly. Mel picked up the nearby feather wand toy and moved it casually in a slow rotation around the floor. Avoiding direct eye contact, Mel continued the slow, steady rhythm, noting Xenia was edging closer and closer. When she could no longer resist the temptation of the feather, Xenia assumed the pounce position. Crouched down, front paws slightly apart, shifting her weight slightly forward and subtly wiggling her butt in the air, she pounced on the unsuspecting toy.

Mel chuckled and continued to entertain her with the toy as we spoke about Xenia's progress since she'd returned;, her relationship with the other Doodlebugs, her unique quirks (including the fact that she liked to pose for the camera!) and her affection for wand toys. They were both watching her and smiling. Mel spoke gently, saying Xenia's name, winning a quick glance from her before her focus returned to the toy.

"I really think she'll do well with Zeke," Mel commented. "We know he'll do well with her; we'll let her adjust and get used to her new brother."

Xenia had made her choice as well, socializing with them openly now. When they sat the carrier on the floor to place her in, Xenia looked around the Manor for a moment, looked at me, and stepped inside. She knew she was on her way to the home she'd waited for. (Give thanks in all circumstances; for this is the will of God in Christ Jesus for you. 1 Thessalonians 5:18)

As we'd all hoped, Xenia and Zeke adjusted well together. Some minor skirmishes over who had dibs on the top shelf of the condo, or who got to the favorite blanket on the couch first were easily overcome as they blended into a family.

Being a part of Xenia's story revealed to me the gift of connection. God's love for us is so great that God provides us with a soul family. God grants us divinely ordained relationships, people and animals, that come into lives at the exact right time.

The circle of love began with Zeke reaching out to form a wonderful brotherly bond with Mick, in the spirit of love and healing. His capacity to share love unselfishly and with his whole heart set the foundation for the soul family, bringing us together, human and animal.

In rescue, despite our best human efforts to secure it, there is no guarantee that an animal will *always* be safe *all* the time. We follow God's direction, understanding that our relationships with others help us heal, forgive, and keep serving as God has called us to do.

Our soul family went on to bless Xenia and bring her into this family. Now her and Mick's soul will be connected even though they never connected here on earth. They are forever family now through love beyond the earthly limitations and into the universal bonds of love.

> For we walk by faith, not by sight. 2 Corinthians 5:7

> Finally, all of you, have unity of mind, sympathy, brotherly love, a tender heart, and a humble mind. 1 Peter 3:8

> So then you are no longer strangers and aliens, but you are fellow citizens with the saints and members of the household of God. Ephesians 2:19

Leonardo

Love Finds a Way

You become responsible, FOREVER, for what you have tamed. —Antoine de Saint-Exupery

We'd been experiencing several days in a row of those dog days of summer with temperatures well above 100 degrees, and no sign of a breeze or break in the heat in the weather forecast. The air hung heavy with humidity, making it a challenge to breathe and warranting heat alerts on the morning news. (Southerners refer to this as 'the air you wear.') Yards were browning all over from the lack of precipitation leaving the area in drought conditions. This type of heat made it difficult to be outside any length of time. If outside exposure was unavoidable, then the key was short trips followed by a hasty return to air conditioning.

"I'm sorry," I responded to the young lady on the phone. "I can barely hear you; can you repeat that?"

She was speaking quietly, and her cell phone kept cutting in and out.

On the other end of the phone was a young lady describing an abandoned male cat trapped outside in this heat with no food, water, or shelter. The cat was stranded outside the food establishment where she waitressed and desperately needed help. The rural area he was in offered very little hope of rescue, so she was reaching out.

"I'm so sorry, I'm struggling to understand you due to our connection," I repeated

A couple moments later, the signal gained strength; However, her voice still held a hushed quality. She apologized, explaining she was calling from outside a local restaurant in a rural small town several miles away. Her need to remain undiscovered by the owner was the reason for her quieted voice.

The owner was forbidding his employees from aiding the cat in any way to discourage him from staying around. He frequently tried shooting him to scare him off and had threatened to call the county shelter to come pick the cat up and get rid of him.

The waitress (Carrie) was concerned and stressed at the urgency of the situation; if she didn't find a shelter to take him in soon, he'd be gone. (Rural county shelters are not where cats want to end up.)

She and the other waitresses were secretly sneaking him food and water after dark to help the poor, lost guy, but it was at the risk of losing their jobs if found out.

Carrie described the cat as friendly and easy-going with everyone he met. He greeted everyone who passed him, rubbing against a leg or attempting to make eye contact. Sometimes, he would follow the patrons right up to the door of the restaurant and proceed trying to accompany them through the door.

As she described the unfortunate circumstance of this poor feline, I put the pieces of his backstory together.

He was obviously used to people, and surely the smell of food was overwhelmingly tempting. He knew the presence of people might mean the offering of a tidbit or scrap of food, and a chance to cool down inside the air-conditioned building.

The cat may have wandered a little far from home and become lost, or accidentally gotten out of someone's car. Far more likely, he'd been dumped by former owners and left to survive on his own, without the necessary skills, in an out of the way location like this. Someone had taught this young cat to depend on humans for his food, shelter, and safety, then abruptly changed their minds, abandoning him in an unfamiliar area.

She continued describing that each time a car would pull up and a door would open, the cat would instantly try to jump inside! There was no doubt he was familiar with people. He was comfortable jumping into a car, associating it with humans. Humans meant food, water, and lodging again. He was looking for the process of survival he'd always known. (He might even be looking for the very home and people who'd driven him here and dumped him.)

My heart sank.

How long had he been here trying to survive on his own, lacking the skills or knowledge to do so? Despite being abandoned, he was still willing to trust humans to help him. *How much longer would he be able to survive out here without shelter, food, or water in the brutal heat of summer?* His chances were slightly more than none. Now the threat of animal control hung over his future.

Considering the situation and the bleak potential future for this fellow (if no one stepped up to assist) I'd already decided we needed to help. My mind was working on the logistics of how to bring this cat to Doodlebug Manor.

"He's such a good cat, ' Carrie continued. "He's been so sweet, and grateful for the scraps we're feeding him. He loves all the attention he can get. Can you please take him in?"

"We'll definitely take him, Carrie," I replied. "Let's figure out how to get him here."

This poor cat was abandoned, all alone and placed at the mercy of people passing him by on their way inside to the air conditioning. No one offered to assist or call for help. Rather, they shooed him away carelessly or kicked at him if he got near their feet. The cat was following his instincts for survival. The cruelty and apathy of the responses he received broke my heart and angered me at the same time. *How could so many ignore the existence and the needs of a fellow soul?*

Our focus became to respond to the urgency of his situation by transferring him into a safe location as soon as possible. From there, we would coordinate the remaining details of transport and receiving him at Doodlebug Manor.

The first few attempts to set it all up fell through, and the frustration and anxiety grew over the need to get to him before animal control was called. One small detail after another fell through as we were racing to get him to safety before he was removed from the restaurant's location. (The first transporter we'd arranged backed out at the last minute; Carrie had agreed to secure the cat but didn't have another shift for two more days.) The pressure to move with haste to see this poor cat to safety was weighing down on us.

I prayed, asking God to show us what was possible, and for Him to remove the obstacles from our path, so we could do the right thing for the cat. It's never a coincidence when pets in need come to us. God put on my heart the love of animals and the desire, above most things, to help them; with His guidance and love, we can. (This God is my strong refuge and he has made my way blameless. 2 Samuel 22:33)

Finally, a viable plan came together, with Carrie agreeing to pick up the cat after dark following her next shift. She would take him home with her for the evening, then meet us at the rendezvous point we'd agreed upon the next day. There were a couple days until her next shift, so to ease the anxiety of waiting, we made the preparations to welcome the new cat on his arrival, and we prayed. Knowing God would provide a way made it bearable.

(Rejoice in hope, be patient in tribulation, be constant in prayer. Romans 12:12)

When Carrie called to confirm she had gotten him, and he was resting safely in her home, I exhaled and offered prayers to thank God.

Arriving a little early at the meeting spot with Carrie, I checked to ensure we had what we needed to transport the new cat home; *Carrier–check, soft towels–check, front carrier door lock–check, Kevlar gloves (in the event we needed them if the cat became spooked or frightened)–check.*

Carrie pulled up beside our car just as I finished my mental checklist. There, sitting contently on her lap while she stroked his fur, was the cat. As she rose to get out of the car, the cat remained calm. Even the noise of the parking lot where we met did not rattle him. He had traveled all this way with no carrier!

Following our greetings to one another, she commented on how well he traveled, and how easy it had been retrieving him the night before. He had spent the night in her bathroom and been a perfect gentleman. We chatted a few minutes more, then I gathered the cat into the carrier I had brought, thanked Carrie for contacting us and her partnership in helping him, and off we went to begin his new life.

Bringing a new cat into the rescue community is always exciting, it's a new chapter starting. Without knowing his past, we didn't know what his reaction to a new environment or a group of mostly younger kittens might be. We had made the commitment to help this poor cat find a second chance, so we would work through whatever occurred.

In preparation for his arrival, I'd placed a large dog cage in the corner equipped with soft blankets, food/water, a litter box, and a couple soft toys for his first night with us. It's a precaution we always take with new incoming cats that provides them with their own space to decompress, feel safe, and become acquainted with their new environment before being introduced to join in.

Entering the Manor, our newest Doodlebug remained calm, and looking around curiously, he exited the carrier easily and entered the cage. He took a couple steps to the center of the cage, then flopped down on the blanket looking content with his new situation.

He was a handsome orange tabby male, about a year or so old, with no obvious wounds or scars. He was thin, but not emaciated. It had been a long couple of days full of changes for him, and after the long car ride he was tired. Having air conditioning and a soft, safe place to lie for the first time in a long time was too good to pass up. His eyes were kind, and his face wore the expression of an animal who has been through a rough time and is realizing that now, for the first time in a while, they are safe. (It's an amazing, soul touching expression.) There was a long exhale as he stretched out across the soft blankets, contentedly closing his eyes. Giving him time to rest, eat something, and start to feel comfortable was the first order of business. We'd check on him again in a bit and plan to become better acquainted.

The kittens were curious about his arrival, gathering around to peer in at the new guy and say hello. A couple of kittens tried reaching through the side of the cage to engage him with a soft paw pat while another tried climbing the side of the cage for a better look. Everyone seemed amiable. There was no aggression or hissing from either side. Truly, the new cat slept through most of the initial kitten mayhem, so we were off to a good start.

My first chance to observe their interaction came the following morning. Opening the door to his cage was our moment of truth. He quietly ambled up to his feet, poked his head out, and moved out of the cage and into the pile of rambunctious kittens who ambushed him on sight. Jumping and running around him, trying to engage him to play with them, Leonardo responded with an easy manner. He flopped down on the floor, rolled over, and batted at them gently, thumping his tail slowly and easily in a patient, content rhythm. Kittens ran up to him, over him, and one even nibbled his ears gently. Leonardo blended in instantly with our existing group.

Taking the opportunity for the first time, I checked out our new Doodlebug more closely for any signs of fleas, ear mites, or injuries, but he appeared whole and healthy. He was a little thin but we would fix that. He was a beautiful deep golden color, with huge eyes that matched his coat color, and crazy long ears. The young cat had three quarters of a tail, and his paws and side flanks were coated in mud. He had a regal face, easy demeanor, and was instantly charming. He looked like royalty and so we dubbed him with the name: Leonardo. This seemed to offer him back some of the well-deserved dignity recent events had attempted to rob him of.

He had been given a good bill of health overall, with one exception; Leonardo tested positive for FIV.

A diagnosis of FIV no longer carried the enigma it once had. Gone were the days this diagnosis was an instant death sentence, or a reason not to adopt. The knowledge that an FIV positive cat could live safely and comfortably with others in a multi-cat environment had become more mainstream. There was no doubt that precautions should always be taken, but for well-adjusted cats in the same home it could work out fine. There was no denying, however, that it could still pose an issue in finding the right home to adopt. While the absolute fear of FIV had eased some in society as the knowledge around it grew, there were still those unsure or afraid of it. FIV+ cats presented a little more challenge in placing him in the right home, but we'd find it.

Being such a charming young cat; it was hard to imagine who would've dumped such a great little soul out in the middle of nowhere, or why. But from the day we brought him into the Manor, he adapted immediately, with no reservations or resentment toward people even after what he'd gone through. Leonardo was just that easy to love. I wondered sometimes how he'd lost the last tip of his tail—or if he'd been born with a shorter tail, but either way it suited him somehow.

Our adoption process continued on through the season, kittens coming in to replace those adopted until the early part of the new year. The adoption season was slowing down for a bit, (post-Christmas season) and things inside the Manor were quiet. We had Leonardo along with a beautiful 6-month-old tabby girl, Jewel, who had arrived late the season before. The two of them were content and got along well, providing companionship for one another. Until the following spring when Jewel was adopted as well, and Leonardo was the last one left of the original group. He kept busy entertaining a new group of kittens in the rescue as they all awaited their adoption days, but it bothered me that he had been passed over so many times.

Leonardo was truly a 1-in-a-million cat. Unfortunately, his FIV diagnosis had made his journey to find the perfect home a little more challenging. My heart hurt for Leonardo, even though he was happy and living his best life with us at the Manor. I wanted more for him, and so we continued seeking the perfect home.

Gregg and I volunteer as needed with a larger scale non-profit national rescue whose emergency rehab facility is in our area, Animal Rescue Corp., Compassion in Action. This group is considered a 'boots on the ground' Emergency Animal Rescue & Disaster Response group[6].

One afternoon, as the rescue transports were being organized, the coordinator mentioned they were two cats short on a transport heading to a large Humane Association in Kentucky. She had arranged for a rescue to take in a couple of FIV cats, but the cats had been adopted by volunteers prior to the transport. That left a couple of spots open for FIV cats! I immediately arranged for Leonardo to take one of the open spots. His opportunity for adoption would be much better in a larger region with more outreach opportunities.

Leaving immediately to gather Leonardo and bring him back, we ensured he was scheduled for the transport leaving early the next morning. We couldn't hesitate to take this opportunity for him, but it meant he was leaving Doodlebug Manor immediately. This was goodbye.

Hugging Leonardo, I described what a wonderful opportunity this was that had come our way. This was his next step to finding his forever home. Smiling, I told him I loved him, and I would miss him terribly, but his forever home was waiting for him. This was the road to his happily ever after; my excitement was contagious.

The reality of releasing this beloved boy didn't settle in until we arrived back at the shelter that afternoon to set him up for transport. I talked to him and reassured him that this was the start of what he'd been waiting for. I set him up in his travel cage with his favorite blanket and toys, a couple treats with his food bowls, and kissed his head. I told him I loved him, and that things would get better and better from here. His forever family was waiting.

Placing a couple of treats in front of him, I watched as he bent to retrieve them, then walked away quickly. Crying as I made my way out of the building, I couldn't look back. (I always cry at goodbye.) As hard as this goodbye was, it was his future awaiting him, and he'd waited long enough.

As I walked away, I prayed God would bring him his happily ever after soon.

Over the course of the next week or so, I spoke with the Humane Association in Kentucky who had taken Leonardo to check up on him. They told me he'd gone to be part of a weekend in-store adoption event and connected me with the adoption coordinator there. As we spoke, she informed me that Leonardo was the hit of the event. He was charming and outgoing, and several people had shown interest in him. By the end of the event, he'd been adopted by a couple who had taken their time to get to know him and adored him.

Leonardo had found his home. His answer came from shared discipleship. It took time to see that the call on my heart from God was successfully carried out. It is within the community of our fellow Christians, by our relationships and their support, that healing ministry can happen. It was through the sharing of complimentary gifts and talents that we were able to serve Leonardo.

Sometimes Christians think in moments like this that if God called them in the privacy of prayer, then it is up to them and them alone. In actuality, though, even if we hear the call alone, we are not meant to carry out the call alone.

Yes, you can decide to follow Christ within your own heart, but to continue to grow in your faith, it takes a community. (Rather, speaking the truth in love, we are to grow up in every way into him who is the head, into Christ, from whom the whole body, joined and held together by every joint with which it is equipped, when each part is working properly, makes the body grow so that it builds itself up in love. Ephesians 4:15-16) It was never God's intention for any of us to live the Christian life alone. The Christian community supports us both individually and together, as we continue to mature and live within the fullness of Christ.

> For where two or three are gathered in my name, there am I among them. Matthew 18:20

> Iron sharpens iron, and one man sharpens another. Proverbs 27:17

Shelby Sue

A Lesson in Joy

"What seems to us as bitter trials are often blessings in disguise." —Oscar Wilde

At first glance, most people might've taken this tiny wisp of a kitten as an orphaned waif, a cast off with ears too large for her head and a wobbly gait. Being a little malnourished with a dullness to her fur, she had ended up here. In fact, most of the people she had encountered in her life up to now had done just that. But they'd missed the true nature of this little Southern charmer. This little girl had been born with a true gentle spirit and possessed the fine art of being able to read the room. With one side glance from her huge green eyes, she could turn on the flirt that would rival Scarlett O'Hara herself. The sparkle in her eye would easily bewitch you when she turned it on.

Our acquaintance began when I reached out to a local 501 (c) (3) animal shelter group that worked to adopt out the pets of a local community shelter. Being new to the area in Southwest Florida, fostering some pets in need seemed like the best place to help while learning about the rescue community and its nuances. So, we began a journey of fostering some pets in need.

The foster outreach team described a kitten who had just arrived ('just' in county shelter terms is a little subjective) as undernourished and alone. She had transferred in from another local shelter after her siblings had all been adopted and she needed some time away from the shelter environment, some one-on-one attention, and TLC to get her healthy and up to weight. So, the order for this little gal was love, food, and attention...my favorite kind of foster.

I picked up the little one, noting she was rail-thin, with the cutest little calico markings. She had a sweet face, muted calico colors on her head and ears. Mostly white, until you reached her little hind quarters where the color burst alive again, just before her disproportionately fluffy tail. Her little head supported huge ears, along with her pretty green eyes, and she had the triangle shaped face of a kitten who is too thin. The foster coordinator told us she came in from another shelter, and the name Shelby had been on her paperwork. After asking the coordinator what else I needed to know about this little waif, we gathered some nutritional kitten food, and off we went to begin our adventure together.

A nice, roomy cage awaited her, complete with all she would need at first, and to provide quarantine for her until we were sure about her health (in response to the sparse health information the shelter had shared). This set-up would also allow our other pets to adjust to the new little presence in their house. We added fresh food and water and a couple of soft toys for snuggling.

We placed her cage in front of the sliding glass doors leading to the lanai in our living room, so she could lie in the sun and watch the woods next to the house for entertainment. In the evenings, she would be with the family to socialize and fit in.

The late morning and afternoon of that first day, she seemed content to sleep on her soft bed in the warmth of a sunbeam shining in on her. She slept soundly. This warm quiet atmosphere was a far cry from the noisy shelter, and she was able to relax and sleep deeply, as most former shelter pets do once they know they are safe. As the afternoon wore on, she awakened a little and began to observe the goings-on around her. By the time evening arrived, her curiosity and desire to be out of a cage and free to explore convinced us to let her out for a little supervised time with us to mingle and get comfortable.

From her first moment of freedom outside her protective cage, she enthralled us all with her outgoing charm. She stepped from her cage to the edge of the couch, tip-toeing over to sit squarely on Gregg's chest. She bumped her nose and purred, rubbing her head against his face. Next, she began to make biscuits and snuggle in, content to be held. She was so willing to give love despite her past, and at the same time possessed an innocent expectation to be loved.

She'd come to us with the name Shelby and while that seemed almost right, it didn't seem quite enough of a name to capture her huge personality. Gregg dubbed her

Shelby Sue, much more befitting a proper Southern kitten. She was the epitome of the expression 'big things coming in small packages.' So, Shelby Sue it was!

We observed that first evening that she was having difficulty walking with a normal gait. Her back right leg dragged slightly behind her and she was unsteady in her movements. She was curious and interested in exploring, but there were clear signs of fatigue. More evident was the absence of any bouts of the 'zoomies' (bursts of energy most kittens exhibit on a moment's notice). She had been through a lot in her short life already, and her state of muscle atrophy due to malnutrition could be what we were seeing expressed. Not knowing for sure what she was experiencing was concerning.

We gave her a few days to rest, settle in, and eat regularly to see if there would be any improvement. When it became clear there was none, I reached back out to the shelter to share my concern and probe for more information about her past and her health record.

This conversation with the cat coordinator revealed that the shelter had spayed her and administered her initial FVCRP vaccinations on the same day she'd arrived. The very day we had picked her up!

I had no words. They elected to spay an underweight, unhealthy kitten and neglected to tell her caretaker? They gave us no warning to watch for post-surgical stress, reactions to the vaccines, no expectation that anesthesia was in her system to explain the lethargy. She was a kitten in recovery, yet no one had bothered to share this information with us to guarantee her best care and outcome.

The irresponsible way the shelter treated a 12-week-old kitten with obvious health concerns was beyond careless. This kitten was at the least a victim of malnutrition (yet they did not test to determine possible cause), was made to endure an invasive surgical procedure she was underweight for, exposed to vaccination serum without proper observation, and still under the influence of anesthesia when released outside the shelter to foster care. Foster care that remained uninformed to any of this, given only instructions to feed her and fatten her up.

Well, at least I left the conversation provided with some knowledge and insight into Shelby's current symptoms. The fatigue, wobbliness, and her hesitance to eat that first day could all be due to what she had just undergone. Luckily, she did not encounter any postoperative issues per se nor any reaction to the vaccinations.

As a few days passed, she still hesitated in eating, taking tiny bites at a time. Her gait remained wobbly and unstable. Her symptoms were beyond shelter shock or anything normal for a kitten of her size and age. The seriousness of her condition was evident, and she needed a medical diagnosis and help.

I made several unsuccessful attempts to reach the shelter foster coordinator, shelter vet, and manager to share my concerns and have her examined. Shelter protocol was to gain permission for the treatment and costs for foster cats, as technically they belonged to the shelter and fell under the shelter's budget. They also reserved the right to make all decisions concerning fosters. (Technically, upon intake, animals are registered with the state, and therefore the shelter is accountable for their whereabouts and condition of life.) When my continued efforts to reach someone to seek help for Shelby Sue landed us nowhere, I loaded her up and took her to our personal vet for an exam. Something was urgently wrong here, and she needed assistance, so I would cover the costs. I had promised to do right by her and protect her when I took her in to foster. That was a promise I was determined to keep.

Following her exam and initial blood work, we went home and waited a couple of days for the results to come in. I prayed and hoped Shelby Sue would have more time to experience life. We prayed God might heal her completely so that she could grow up and be a part of our family where she fit in beautifully and was already loved. We asked the Lord to show us the right path to care for this precious soul.

When the test results came back, it revealed that Shelby Sue had compromised kidneys. X-rays revealed kidney failure (CKD).

The unusual shape and size of both her kidneys, much smaller than a typical kitten, led the vet to suspect the cause could be hereditary. She had been born with the compromise. If this was not hereditary in a kitten her age, a traumatic event was the next most common cause of CKD in kittens. (The consumption of antifreeze is a major cause of cat poisoning that can cause renal disease or kidney failure.) Most times, kittens would not survive these traumas.

It was difficult to say for sure what caused this in the absence of the results from a specific (CKD) blood test panel to identify the values in her system. (CKD tests measure the BUN or urea, creatinine and SDMA), potassium and sodium, magnesium, proteins in the blood (albumin and globulin), and other readings that are often out of range in CKD cats (cholesterol, ALT, amylase, glucose and CK). The tests are similar to those performed on humans with the same ailments.

The hard reality was CKD was not something that could be cured.

We might prolong her time and give her a better quality of life, but there was simply no way to know how long she might be with us. Certainly, if it was a poisoning, it would considerably shorten her life expectancy.

CKD is an ailment most often seen in older cats, making it difficult for the veterinarian to speculate on her life expectancy. (In fact, it is all too common in older cats.) She might live a few years or a few months. If she responded to treatment protocol, it might improve her quality of life based on the responses they had seen in older cats. Kidney disease treatment in cats is managed mostly with medications, diet, supplements, and hydration. Specific management is geared toward the underlying cause and the stage of the disease. Having no knowledge of her history, the test might at least shed some light on the cause and stage of the disease we were dealing with.

The vet referred us back to the shelter for the in-depth blood testing since the kitten was a foster and technically they 'owned' the responsibility for her, but also shared with us that the shelter had been the recipient of several donated blood testing kits through a grant, so it would cost them nothing to perform (in place of the vet's office where more substantial lab charges could apply which we would cover.)

The choices were difficult: *Did we put her through another blood panel test to gather what information we could? Did we opt to forgo the testing and begin the treatment plan with her, since it would be a similar plan either way? Could we even consider taking on this disease without at least an idea of what we were looking at?*

I reached out to the cat coordinator who had arranged our foster to secure the test. We endured the waiting for results and offered prayers for this sweet little soul. We knew enough of the facts to know the situation didn't look good for Shelby Sue, but God could do all things, and so we prayed for the very best possible outcome.

I began researching everything I could find about CKD in cats. I watched YouTube and checked veterinarians' websites. I learned about special diets and supplements, holistic additives, how to administer IV Fluids, and began the regime with Shelby Sue. I consulted with trusted veterinarians I had worked with for years in Tennessee for ideas and advice. I learned and listened, but the fact remained there was very little information that dealt with the treatment of CKD in kittens. Some of the advice was even contradictory regarding advice for care and nutrition. (Most prevalent was the discussion on whether to feed CKD cats/kittens foods high in protein to nourish them or with no protein to protect the kidney function they did have.)

The results of the blood test through the shelter were texted back to me, and so we turned back to our vet for the prognosis. He interpreted her values from the testing and the news was not what we'd hoped. We discussed the management plan with the vet and learned there were a whole series of additional tests we could run, but the diagnosis would not change.

So, we moved forward knowing the best we could do was provide her with the best care possible and love her daily, praying for the best. We would make our time with this little angel happy and enjoy her wonderful little spirit, continuing to pray for guidance.

Armed with the information and what Shelby Sue was up against, I attempted again to contact the shelter manager several times with no response. Finally, weary of making no progress, I placed a call to the dog coordinator's on-call cell phone to have the manager paged.

Surprisingly, the moment the manager took the phone she began a loud verbal assault directed at me personally. She began by listing all the things I had done wrong around Shelby Sue's care and seemed convinced that I was challenging her authority over the kitten. She was angry that I had found help for Shelby Sue without her permission. She seemed most angry at my having taken her to a vet outside the shelter.

I struggled to remain calm and reasonable, explaining the circumstances, although I was shaking with anger at this point. Still, I tried to keep my voice steady and appropriate in tone. Most appalling to me was her absolute absence of concern for the kitten. As I explained, I had absorbed the costs because I had sought help. She became worse. It was clear very quickly that she was most concerned that I had threatened her authority in my attempt to save the kitten. Despite my attempts to explain the situation honestly, she wasn't prepared to listen. The conversation was deteriorating quickly; she demanded I return Shelby Sue to the shelter that afternoon.

This was not an option.

Returning Shelby Sue would mean a certain death by euthanasia for this sweet kitten at a county shelter. They would not pursue saving a 12-week-old kitten with a terminal illness, which would mean returning her to the lack of care or concern they had demonstrated all along in the worst of circumstances. We had already fallen in love with this precious soul and I would find a better way to resolve this confrontation so that Shelby Sue came out the winner.

Thinking quickly, and with a steely determination, I persuaded her to allow us to adopt Shelby Sue. We would adopt her, and the issue would be resolved for the manager since she would be marked as adopted and no longer the shelter's responsibility. We agreed I would return their cat carrier to them and sign the papers for her adoption that afternoon. I also resigned over the phone from any further volunteering or fostering with that shelter. I could not fathom working for a shelter with so little concern for the pets they were supposed to be caring for.

As the conflict reached a resolution, the manager offered to waive Shelby Sue's usual adoption fee, to which she alluded was a concession on her part to be nice. It's important to note that they could be held in violation of state health codes and animal related guidelines for releasing an obviously ill kitten into foster care, refusing to be available to provide followup care, and then adopting out a kitten with a confirmed terminal illness. I took the offer and by the end of the afternoon, Shelby Sue was officially adopted into our family.

With this nonsense behind me, we were overjoyed to welcome Shelby Sue as a permanent member of our pack.

Now she was home for good. She had already come into our lives, set a place for herself, charming us all, and winning our hearts.

We planned to share the good news and slowly began her introductions with our pets. Shelby Sue had never met a stranger and was already casting her spell over our dog, Ollie. Ollie was stretched out in the sun on the lanai next to the pool when Shelby Sue walked right up to him and began rubbing against his tall legs and purring. She head butted him repeatedly, finally collapsing down to lie with him, tangled in the whiskers of his muzzle! This tiny kitten had literally crawled onto his warm face to nestle in. This was the beginning of a very tight-knit, sweet friendship. From their initial meeting forward, anytime Shelby would see Ollie, she would run on her little wobbly legs to get to him with incredible determination. She would snuggle right into her favorite spot on his face if he were laying down or stretched out in the sun. Ollie always tolerated whatever form of affection Shelby Sue brought him. They were buds.

The other cats took a little more time to win over, but they were no match for Shelby Sue. She was determined to love and to be loved. Her aura was like a bright, happy halo she cast all around.

Her next conquest was our oldest cat, Rascal. She was a van tabby with mostly white fur, bright and clean looking like new fallen snow, with some very notable black spots scattered intermittently across her torso. All leading to a solid black matching tail that looked tacked onto her rump area. The most notable spot Rascal had resembled a toupee that had been dropped on the top of her head, sitting a little forward and looking like rather short bangs from the back. The toupee was punctuated on either side by her beautiful pink ears, adding an endearing quality. The hallmark feature of Rascal's face was the solid black coloring that covered her nose from the bridge (squarely centered between her eyes) to the bottom of her nose leather. Her name had been earned from the time she arrived as a rescue kitten herself some 16 years ago. She was a precocious kitten from the start, with an uncanny talent for finding her way from one mishap to another. Being adventurous, mischievous, and unapologetic were her greatest talents.

Little had changed over the years. She had established herself among the other cats as the clan matriarch. While she thought of herself as no nonsense and in charge, her tough facade did not fool the other cats, including Shelby Sue. At this age, her favorite way to spend her days was lying on her pillow (and only *her* pillow) on the lanai in the sun, enjoying the outdoor sights and sounds. She would only consent to come inside at sunset due to our unrelenting insistence.

Shelby Sue had wasted no time spotting the pillow with the larger cat occupying it, unassumingly crawling up onto it to snuggle in as close as she dared to Rascal's warm, comforting back. While she met her with some hissing and fussing, Shelby Sue stayed true to the course and would not leave. Not even the warning, in the form of a pop on the head, would daunt this effervescent kitten. It was entertaining to watch the space between them shrink with each attempt until Shelby Sue had worked her way right up against Rascal without an inch between. As long as no one took notice of it, the snuggling would be tolerated. We laughed at how much alike they looked sleeping side by side earning them the nickname "Me and Mini Me."

Zaeus was the easy-going guy in the group, an orange tabby with a loving disposition. Shelby Sue seemed to gravitate toward him, as she had with Ollie, and follow him around like a little sister. Where he went, she would go. Their relationship took a little work at first, as Zaeus would allow her to approach him and even a face rub or two, but as she would walk by, he would sniff her backside and hiss and push her away. Clearly, he could tell she was ill, and his natural instincts as a cat were to shun her. After a few encounters, seeing she was here to stay, her adoration was too much for him to resist. His hesitation melted as it was no match for the gentle charms of Shelby Sue and her big heart. Zaeus gave in to the role of big brother and began mentoring her in the skills of lizard hunting on the lanai, a favorite sport of cats in Florida.

Shelby Sue was a quiet girl with soft steps and a gentle approach. Occasionally she would converse in tiny, barely audible mews. Still, generally, her greetings were a head bump with a flash of big green eyes. The only exception to this mannerism was when she would spot Ollie or Zaeus (or both) on the lanai, prompting her to run with all she was worth meowing at them to wait for her. These were her boys, her pack. That was part of the allure of Shelby Sue; she was happy to love everyone and so joyful. When she was alone on the lanai, she would occupy her time chasing bugs and lizards, sometimes watching the surrounding woods with the intensity and concentration only a cat exhibits. She would stretch out and nap in the sun, warm and content.

We all settled into a happy little routine early with Shelby Sue. She seemed content to have a comfortable place where she belonged and was loved, giving love and joy in return. Things had started off a little rough for her in life, but you'd never know it now that she had found a home and a family to belong to. She had really come into our home content just to be there.

Shelby Sue was a trooper as her daily feeding routine became a series of syringe feedings, Sub Q fluids, and nutritional paste for energy. She ingested probiotics, and immune boosts, a balanced diet of Kidney Care food in as much quantity as her little system would tolerate. She took it all in stride as a part of everyday life.

Her nickname, "Sugar Pie," evolved so naturally from her persona that it stuck. We would sing "Sugar Pie, Honey Bunch" to her during the day while we spent hours with her beside us. She continued to romp in the sun on the lanai with her 'boys,' and sat beside me in the kitchen while we mixed her kitten food cocktails. She spent her evenings snuggled on a blanket on the couch or nestled on Gregg's chest in front of the TV. As she tired out, she'd curl up in her soft, donut-style bed on the couch near Ollie, having foregone the cage for sleeping in weeks ago. In the mornings, we'd come out to find her eager to begin the next day with us, meowing at the glass doors of the lanai to go outside. This was the routine as we enjoyed the summer and time spent with this beautiful kitten. We treasure it still.

As the summer ended, so did the happy days for Shelby Sue, giving way to listlessness. The joy she naturally radiated was less and less as she favored sleep over everything else. She grew weaker; doing the things she loved most became a struggle.

It was a reasonably quick decline, and the morning her breathing became labored, we knew: It was time to release Shelby Sue from the body she'd been born into that had let her down. She had fought valiantly against the odds, experienced her time as a kitten with a happy, loving spirit. But the joy that filled her days now had waned, and it was time to let her be free, to send her back to the Lord.

We had never intended to adopt another pet, but Shelby Sue was not just another pet. This tiny girl had walked right into our lives with an amazing spirit brimming with love and acceptance. We had all fought vigilantly, determined to give Shelby Sue a place she belonged where she was loved and could enjoy the time she'd been given. Against all odds, this sweet girl had an indomitable spirit and had found her peace despite the challenges life had dealt her.

She was an inspiration, the way her spirit embraced each day with hope and excitement to see what was next. Despite her challenges, she reveled in the sunshine and lived in each moment and the joy of the Lord. We too have the power to choose to revel in the sunshine despite the darkness that occasionally abounds.

It's been a while since we had to say goodbye to our little Sugar Pie. It is still hard to recount the loss without some tears, but now whenever we think of her, we smile and feel that bright spirit and a warm glow in our hearts.

If things had gone as expected at so many steps along the way, we might never have known Shelby Sue. She might never have gotten to shine her light into the world, and we wouldn't carry the love in our hearts for this exceptional little soul. God had taken what could have been bad circumstances for this sweet soul, turning them again and again into something wonderful. (My times are in your hand; rescue me from the hand of my enemies and from my persecutors! Psalm 31:15)

Until we see you again Shelby Sue, keep shining in Heaven.

> For everything there is a season, and a time for every matter under heaven: Ecclesiastes 3:1
>
> May the God of hope fill you with all joy and peace in believing, so that by the power of the Holy Spirit you may abound in hope. Romans 15:13

Falco & Vinny

It's All Good

God does not call the equipped, He equips the called
—Anonymous

Initially, cats were welcomed into human society as the relationship proved mutually beneficial between cats and men; cats hunted mice and other rodents, keeping communities and their storehouses of food relatively free of these pests. In turn, the cats were fed, housed, and offered companionship. Some cultures worshiped cats for all their virtues. You can see the evidence of this today contained in the Egyptian hieroglyphs: in particular, the Goddess Bastet. Another commonly seen token of cats is the Japanese 'Waving Cat' or Maneki-neko believed to bring good luck to its owner.

Throughout time and in many cultures, cats have been worshiped, honored, viewed as tokens of luck and prosperity, and considered ushers into the spiritual world. However, over the years, their affiliation with some holidays and taboo practices has left an enigma on the reputation of cats, in particular the black cat. While many cat enthusiasts recognize the beauty and poise of our ebony feline friends, they are often subject to scrutiny or misconception affiliated with the more sinister stereotypes and folklore. Even in modern times, black cats often bear the enigmas assigned to them through the years.

I was a fairly new volunteer, fostering with a local nonprofit group tied to the local county animal shelter in SW Florida. We had recently relocated to the area, so fostering with them provided a nice break from the business of running a full-time, full-scale rescue and allowed me time to work with the animals and enjoy them. That's always been my favorite part, building relationships and bonds with the animals.

Stopping into the shelter one afternoon, Linda, one of the cat room coordinators, greeted me and we chatted. Visiting with the adoptable cats inside the kennels, Linda shared some details around each one, focusing on the ones who might benefit from foster care. There were young and old cats, new arrivals and longtime residents, all with various backgrounds and their own unique story.

When we reached the last cage in the row, it was difficult to see who was inside. It was a dark, quiet cage at floor level, requiring extra effort to peer inside. (The preferred cages are mid-level, in the 'line of sight' of potential adopters when they enter the room.)

Moving in closer, it was still difficult to see the inhabitant of this cage, though I saw a flicker from a set of large, bright green eyes staring out at me from the back corner. A hefty tag on the front of his cage read 'Falco' and had the shelter's designation for 'special needs.'

The inhabitant turned out to be a small, short-haired, male black cat. He sat hunched back as far as he could into the back corner of his cage, gazing out. His demeanor was timid and evasive, not outgoing or attention seeking, like so many cats hoping for a bit of attention. Instead, he seemed to recoil and shrink back from any movement by his cage, afraid of anything that might interrupt his quiet solitude inside.

Recognizing my interest in this small, withdrawn cat, Linda told me the story of Falco, emphasizing that he was a special needs case indeed. One in desperate need of foster care.

He had arrived on a transfer to the shelter at the young age of 8 weeks from another shelter. Early on, it was apparent there was something not quite right. Falco had notable neurological challenges even as a baby, but what they were and how severe was undetermined. Falco faced a double challenge: he was a black cat with no distinguishing features and special needs. (Even today, black cats are the least often adopted from shelters and rescues, making them the most frequently euthanized.)

Falco had been diagnosed with CH, Cerebellar Hypoplasia, but his level of impairment had not been determined. **Cerebellar hypoplasia** is a developmental condition in which the brain's cerebellum fails to develop properly. The cerebellum, the portion of the brain that controls fine motor skills, balance, and coordination, affects the cat's ability to function 'normally.' This most commonly occurs when a pregnant cat becomes infected with feline panleukopenia virus and passes the infection to her unborn kittens. The severity of the symptoms depends on how much of the cerebellum was affected and at what stage of development the infection occurred. Other causes can include being born to a mother who is severely malnourished during her pregnancy or if the kitten suffers a physical trauma to its brain. The condition is not painful or contagious.

His arrival here at the cooperative nonprofit affiliate of the county shelter afforded him the opportunity to be assessed and determine his quality of life. This, in turn, would decide his fate. Originally, the shelters board determined that euthanasia of such a small kitten was not the proper course. Instead, they decided to care for Falco and allow him to continue to grow and develop while monitoring his condition. That was over 7 months ago.

Still a kitten, Falco had existed for most of his life up to now inside an 18' x 22' steel cage on the bottom of a stack of metal cat kennels. The cage was dark, with reduced visibility to the potential adopters who came through looking for their next pet. The cages were fully exposed to the traffic shuffling through the room with no option for privacy or peace. His life had been devoid of the attention and love any kitten needs, let alone one with special needs.

He'd had very little life experience outside this cage, making him effectively a prisoner in solitary confinement.

Attached to the cat adoption room was an area where the cats could have time outside their cages playing and interacting with people. It was challenging to find volunteers who would take him to the playroom. Due to the symptoms of his disability, it was apparent to the volunteers his time spent there was traumatic and frightening to Falco. This meant he received very little time outside his cage, and the continual confinement contributed to his fear when he left.

He needed a foster home with one-on-one time, concentrated care, and a full assessment of his ability to adapt and have a quality life. If someone would take the time to build a bond, and create trust with Falco, he stood a chance of being coaxed out of his shell and into a real life.

"Would you be willing to foster him?" Linda asked me. "Just to try to work with him?"

I had worked with a couple 'neuro' kitties in the past and have a weak spot for them, but this was a huge responsibility into unknown territory. I had no knowledge of CH, nor had I ever taken on the responsibility of a cat disabled by this condition. My heart went out to Falco. This kitten just needed a chance.

That's when I heard the small inner voice speaking to me; *This kitten was given life, but has he lived any of it, while stuck inside that dark, lonely cage? What was a life apart from sunlight and love, all the blessings and experiences life had to share? He had yet to experience most of that. He'd been here 7 months, and no one had invested any time to help him, or test the limits of what he could achieve, disability or not. Could he have a happy existence? Didn't he deserve the chance to try?*

This would be a new challenge and different responsibility than I'd ever taken on before. It essentially amounted to life or death for Falco. This would be his trial run in the real world, to see if he could function and have a quality life. *Was I qualified to help him and lead him to success?*

The shelter would use our time together to measure his adaptability and potential. I wanted to ensure I was up to the challenge, and would be helping this cat, not giving him more empty promises.

"I'd like to help him, Linda," I told her. "Let me consider it over the weekend and get back to you."

That evening, I talked over the situation with Gregg. What were his thoughts? Would I be able to do this? What if I tried and failed, and it effectively ended his life? How would I feel about providing long-term foster for a disadvantaged cat that might be with us a while before adoption? Would anyone ever adopt him?

Gregg listened to my concerns. We discussed each point, and in the end, he shared his thoughts: "No one else is stepping up to help him. You would at least be giving him a chance at life. If anyone can do this Lara, you can."

Recognizing that the small inner voice in my head was a call from God, and with Gregg's support and encouragement, I wanted to do this, but was afraid.

I prayed, confessing my fears of failure and uncertainty to God. This was a big undertaking; one I did not feel qualified for. God had called me, and my spirit would not be able to walk away from this little soul in need. Expressing my willingness to follow the call, I asked God for his guidance. (Let not your hearts be troubled. Believe in God; believe also in Me. John 14:1)

Calling the shelter back the next morning, I arranged to meet with Falco and determine what the situation was. I chose to meet on Sunday, the day the shelter was closed to the public so it would be quiet, and we could get acquainted slowly, on his time.

When the volunteer brought him into the cat playroom, she shared their knowledge about him; it wasn't much but, it was a starting point.

"Try to avoid making any loud noises," she said. "And be careful not to make any sudden movements. It tends to startle him and rile him up."

Falco was released from the cat carrier into the playroom, and from the start, he was frantic and unsure of what was happening. Struggling to get his bearings, he was scared, but doing his best to focus on his new surroundings. Scampering from one corner to the next, he sought a safe place to hide while he absorbed what was happening. This new environment and temporary freedom were overwhelming for him. Sensing the energy of the rooms around him, and the scents left by other cats in the room and on the toys, was a form of sensory overload.

I chose a spot on the floor in the corner and sat down. I greeted Falco with a happy, calm energy. I spent the beginning of our time just talking with him, letting him get used to the calmness in my voice. As his agitation subsided, I slowly moved the feather wand toy back and forth across the floor to engage him. He watched the rhythm of the movement, then while safely outside my grasp, began to paw at it. This was a sign of hope. If Falco could be removed from the noise, scents, exposure of other cats, and chaos of a shelter, he might just relax and learn to be happy.

I wasn't convinced I knew the path to help this young cat, but any attention and love would be better than what he was experiencing now. So, armed with some supplies from the shelter, and trusting God would guide us both, we bundled Falco into a cat carrier and off we went to start a new journey together. (And we know that for those who love God all things work together for good, for those who are called according to his purpose. Romans 8:28)

"We're in this together, buddy," I told Falco on the ride home. "I'll help you if you help me. We can do this."

It was trial-and-error the first few days. I spent a lot of time just 'being there' with him and speaking to him while observing his movements and learning to interpret them. Letting him get acclimated and comfortable in the rescue cottage was an essential first step.

Soothing, soft music played in the background. There were plenty of comfortable beds and blankets with soft, snuggly toys, and his eating area was set up in proximity for him to get to quickly. Careful to keep the center of the floor clear, to avoid any tripping hazards and to allow him ample room to move and explore, we'd set his area up along the back and side walls. This also seemed to help him find his bearings in the first few days. Keeping a progress journal, I notated every discovery along the way.

Meanwhile, I researched CH online, finding several sources of information about the disorder, typical symptoms, and ideas on how to accommodate Falco's needs. One special Facebook group of CH cat owners worldwide offered advice, insights, ideas, and tips for caring for CH cats. Primarily, this group provides support and encouragement to one another and those new to caring for CH cats. The group is called ***Cerebellar Hypoplasia Cats & Kittens***[7].

Falco's symptoms were among those most common in CH cats. His eyes weren't coordinated well enough to focus clearly. He could track movement, and would see large or reflective objects, but his depth perception was deceiving. In response, he would reach out toward an item, but his movements were jerky and wild in appearance. His reach resulted in a wide-ranging batting motion in the air. He struggled to maintain his balance, and his right back leg would turn underneath him if he placed any weight on it, effectively turning him, or causing a small collapse. He could walk awkwardly, sometimes with a slight wobble, but he never gave up. If startled or in a hurry, he would wobble with his front legs doing most of the work, and his back leg landing hard behind him, making a slapping sound. He did experience mild head tremors from time to time, but nothing was pronounced.

I wondered in my heart if he even knew this was a disability? He certainly didn't let it slow him down, and he'd never known anything different. Truthfully, having been cooped up in a cage with little room to move for so many months, this may've been more about freedom than execution to him. If he didn't realize it was a disability, I certainly wasn't going to treat him like it was.

Once he was comfortable settling in, we began setting up routines to make things easy and predictable for him. Each time I entered the cottage, I called his name in a happy, friendly tone and continued to chat with him. At mealtimes, I would use a specific call to announce it was chow time, which he learned to identify quickly. When he was relaxed in his blanket, I would gently approach, letting him sniff my hand to learn my scent, then gently rub the side of his face. We would introduce toys he could chase or watch. (His favorite toy was the electronic 'catch a mouse' that twirled a fur covered wand in random motion from underneath a cloth cover. This toy engaged him and helped him to focus on the wand to catch the twirling mouse.) The catch a mouse toy time was the event that elicited the first meow we heard from Falco, music to my ears!

A standard litter box provided a challenge for Falco, as the rim was too rigid for him to negotiate, and his balance made it difficult to stand inside. Litter would get stuck between his toes, and sometimes he would miss all together. After several iterations and combinations, we found what worked best for him, and then stuck with it. A simple cookie sheet with potty training pads, placed in the corner with a guide rail made of an old plastic litter bucket, provided a 'stall' that helped provide stability when he lost his balance.

Falco was an intelligent cat; he learned quickly and retained what he learned. He didn't give up. Anything he set out to do, he would continue to try until he achieved it. We might change the approach or find a way to enable him beyond what a 'normal' cat would do, but he did it. It looked like we were on to something here: time, love, and attention seemed to be the keys to Falco's success.

He had a sweet temperament, was laid back and patient as we tried new things, but certainly he had his own likes and dislikes. Falco liked having the side of his face petted, and sometimes his sides or belly. He did not want anyone getting too close to his food dish. In his attempt to defend it, he would go to it, batting wildly at the air above it until he felt like any perceived threat had passed. This was his attempt to 'scent' his dish and the surrounding area with his paw, as normal cats would do to claim their territory. His focus off, he would continue to ' scent ' until he was satisfied he'd claimed it. He required extra maintenance on grooming, mostly washing his feet and between his toes to remove the leftover bits of food that would get stuck there. (Falco loved mealtimes most of all and, in his excitement, he would often step into his plate. He didn't always catch the extra bits between his toes.) He would tolerate some assistance in cleaning, but when it went on too long, I'd receive a quick, firm slap of the paw. This was 'no' from Falco.

Falco was adapting beautifully. The patience granted to allow him to adjust to this new world outside a cage, TLC, and new fun experiences were paying off. Falco was more than capable of living a life of quality and happiness; he was doing it! Any fears around this were quelled. It was a blessing and heartrending to watch this cat come into his own.

The next step in his development would determine how he would do with another kitten/cat. This could be a considerable aid in his potential to find a home. Since Falco had missed out on the crucial learning and bonding opportunities kittens develop at an early age among one another, it was essential to his development. He needed the chance to be around others of his species, to learn and grow, and to have the potential for companionship. No more loneliness locked up in a cage on his own.

A play date was set with a fellow foster and her 3-month-old kitten to see how they would do together. This was an excellent opportunity for both kittens to socialize and to measure how Falco would do with another cat coming into this space. Falco was fascinated and watched as the kitten explored and played. At first, he was a little unsure but never showed any aggression or territorial tendencies toward the other kitten. That was a great sign Falco could most likely adapt to another cat.

I shared the news of all the progress Falco was making with the Foster Coordinator. Adding in my desire to pair another kitten with him in foster to improve his potential to bond to another cat. Not long after, she contacted me about an 8-week-old kitten, with a trauma to his right eye, who would benefit from fostering. We were excited to bring him in, to help with his medical needs, and to allow Falco a kitten, a companion, and a friend.

An eye infection that hadn't been caught in time had compromised the kitten's right eye, and he stood to lose it as a result. Once he reached the age to be neutered, the shelter would do both surgeries at once. In the meantime, we would treat his eye and administer medicine to ward off any complications or further infection.

Vinny was a small, gray tabby with an outgoing, playful temperament. Nothing slowed him down; he had endless energy. He bounded up the cat condo and jumped from the shelves to the counters and back to the floor with no issues. He was interested in everything.

The first meeting on the evening Vinny joined us was a little tense. Vinny was unsure about this larger kitten with some strange behaviors, but he was curious. He hissed and arched his back, but to no avail. Falco made no move to be confrontational, but instead charged over to defend his food bowl from this new intruder. He set to work immediately, fumbling and swiping the air directly over the food to stake his claim. Unfortunately, this only drew Vinny's interest, intensifying Falco's thwarted attempts to defend it. To set things back on track, I walked to the food bowl a couple feet away and shook it, calling Vinny. This was his area, set far enough away to save poor Falco from going into spasms at every meal.

Any tension between the two was short-lived, however. It didn't take Vinny long to realize the perks of having another kitten to play with. He'd decided that Falco would make the ideal big brother and set about making it happen. Whatever Vinny was doing seemed to work. Around two days after his arrival, I walked into the Manor to give the boys breakfast, and found Vinny curled up asleep, snuggled into Falco, with Falco's arms around him. Within less than a week, they became inseparable!

That memory still makes my heart swell. These two were bonding, which was exactly what each of them needed. They had each other.

Vinny was instrumental in introducing movement and noise, and new toys into Falco's world. All with positive results. This is what Falco's life has become now. These two boys spent their days and nights being kittens and were bonded brothers.

The day of Vinny's scheduled surgery (eye removal and neuter) Falco was uneasy without his buddy. The entire day, he fretted and seemed distraught until the late afternoon when Vinny returned. Vinny was tired and a little cranky from the anesthesia at first, but they were curled up together again by bedtime. The bond these two sweet boys formed was the making of them both. Falco finally had the chance to be a cat, and both Falco and Vinny had a family. They would need to be adopted together.

Because Falco and Vinny were both considered 'special needs' cats, when they were ready to be adopted, we reached back to the international CH group on social media that had been so helpful and told their story. They were instrumental in helping us spread the word about Falco and Vinny needing a home together.

The response we received was quicker than we'd expected, and they were adopted together into a beautiful home located just under 40 minutes away from us. An outstanding Veterinary Technician had been looking to adopt and care for a special needs cat, and when she read the story of Falco and Vinny, she was convinced they were the ones for her.

Falco and Vinny found their happily ever after. In part, maybe even due to what was once a disability for both, and a journey of discovery together.

God's whisper in my ear, the 'small inner voice' guiding me to help a forgotten little soul in the corner of a cat room, was a blessing waiting to happen. It was a wonderful, gratifying experience, both teaching and learning from Falco and Vinny as we navigated together through uncharted waters with God's guidance.

Once I took the first step to trust, my confidence grew through prayer and my spiritual equipping came in all sorts of forms. God provided us with all we needed to succeed: the knowledge that Falco was there and in need, the knowledge around CH, an excellent kitten companion and friend through Vinny. He led the way to an international group of experienced and supportive CH cat owners and provided a home together for the boys, a home that existed just up the road from us, and the perfect adopter He sent, a Veterinary Technician with the knowledge and desire to love and care for them. It was all God once I leaned in and trusted Him.

Just because you are afraid to serve does not mean you should be afraid to answer God's call. When God calls you, God will guide you; you are not alone.

> And I heard the voice of the Lord saying, "Whom shall I send, and who will go for us?" Then I said, "Here am I! Send me." Isaiah 6:8
>
> It is the Lord who goes before you. He will be with you; he will not leave you or forsake you. Do not fear or be dismayed. Deuteronomy 31:8

Heidi Lou

High Speed Foster

Every cat is my best friend. —Unknown

I peeked inside the carrier to see two bright green almond-shaped eyes and a sea of gray velvet. Val was making her way through the door with our new foster kitten, food supplies, and a baggie of toys. I reached out to assist her in carrying some bulky items to lighten her load.

Val was the Foster Care Coordinator for the local rescue where we volunteered to foster. She was a woman small in stature, with a vast capacity to love. She was retired, widowed, and living her best life, working to coordinate all the foster care and caregivers for the cats affiliated with St. Francis Rescue in the area.

This was the beginning of our latest foster adventure: Heidi. She had been in foster for a few weeks with another volunteer who needed the space to care for a couple of special needs kittens, so we agreed to take over the care of Heidi until she was ready to be adopted. The day a new foster cat arrives is always exciting, like Christmas morning! I was eager to get a look at our newest friend. (Fostering is like getting to experience the joy and excitement of adopting a new pet each time a new cat is entrusted into our care. We love, care for, socialize them, and then transition them to prepare for their adoptive homes.)

We'd relocated from Middle Tennessee to Southwest Florida, into a secured neighborhood with certain HOA restrictions on pets. This environment would not support operating a rescue as we had done so many years prior. This was the perfect opportunity to continue our ministry to help God's animals by providing foster care for a local rescue. Fostering cats on behalf of a rescue helps to free precious space inside the shelters. It's a crucial part of the rescue process, ensuring those already under the care of the rescue are safe and cared for while allowing the rescue or shelter to continue to reach out to those in need of a safe place. This creates the quintessential 'win-win-win' all the way around.

Many smaller shelters and rescues are constantly looking to find people interested in helping in this way for all types of pets. Fostering is a life-saving mission.

For anyone interested in adopting, especially first-time adopters, fostering provides great hands-on experience and an opportunity to find the exact 'match' for your home! It's as easy as reaching out to inquire about foster programs with reputable rescues. Most rescuers love what is often called 'foster failures.' (Some rescue folks use the term to describe a pet taken in as a foster who ends up adopted by their foster family. I'm always puzzled by this 'backward' term, as finding the best home for each pet adopted is the goal, not a failure!) Generally, the term is meant to be tongue in cheek, and is most commonly referring to a foster that was intended to stay in foster care from the start. Still, the animal wins their heart and becomes a family member.

We walked the carrier to my office (foster room) and sat it down to let Heidi get oriented and explore. Our foster room was decked out with a tall cat condo, a toy box with an assortment of playthings, smaller cardboard scratchers, and an area set apart for their litter box. Additionally, we had lined the shelves inside the room's closet with baskets made of soft weave material they could climb into and snuggle inside to nap. Directly across from the closet, the front wall of the room had floor to ceiling windows letting in ample sunshine and overlooking the front landscaping, complete with views of the hibiscus shrubs and the lizards who lived within them! The cats loved to curl up in the 'sunshine puddles' and nap or watch the birds through the windows.

Heidi resembled a classic painting, with her beautiful, solid gray coat, from head to toe. Her fur was short, thick, and velvety, stretching down the length of her from the tip of her head down her long tail. Even her nose pad and jellybean toes were a matched shade of gray. Her face was thin, with slightly large pointy ears, exotic green eyes, and long white whiskers. She was svelte and graceful and looked almost fluid when she walked. Winding around the base of the cat condo to get her scent on it, she stopped to stretch out her arms and dig her claws in to scratch the sisal rope. She was a stretch cat, the kind that seem to get incredibly long when they stretch out. Heidi seemed so long and thin that I wondered where the rest of her went when she stood up!

She didn't waste a moment being demure. She darted out of the carrier to begin her exploration. Heidi was vivacious, curious, and set about learning the entire room.

Val and I stepped out to review her history and vetting schedule for the coming weeks. It always worked well to know the schedule ahead of time (days she'd be going to get vaccines or for checkups and, of course, her spay appointment.) This was also a great opportunity to learn more about each specific kitten's behavioral quirks or preferences to gain a head start on their care. Generally, any health issues are a point of discussion before the placement of kittens with fosters, to ensure the foster home is prepared to work with the kittens' needs and have the right experience to do so.

Heidi quickly became Heidi-Lou; it just suited her better. She had an interesting tendency toward a tomboy attitude. She climbed everything in sight and introduced herself to our older cats. She was proving to be a very entertaining, energetic, and friendly kitten during her first days with us. (Dubbed 'High Speed' by Gregg, she could give the old 'Energizer Bunny' from the battery commercials a run for his money!) She ran in high gear from when she awoke in the morning to the nighttime.

She could find entertainment in everything from a toy tossed for her retrieval (Yes, Heidi loved to play 'fetch') to a speck of dust she might spy falling in a sunlight beam. She was incredibly charming and won our hearts quickly.

We had started socializing early, letting her spend her days and evenings out with the family, including our 3 older cats and our dog, Ollie. She was outgoing, only wanting our gang to play with her and accept her. The only danger was, now and then, when she was insistent they play with her, she might irritate our older cats intent on taking their naps. Heidi-Lou had a replenishing source of energy with small, instant breaks in-between. She played hard, until she couldn't take another step, and would drop where she was to catch a brief nap, and then she was off and running again. (Most kittens can stop and sleep, even in mid-play, but Heidi-Lou was never down long!)

In the evenings, we tossed spring toys for her to hunt. This would go for some time until we could coax her to lie down on the soft blanket for a neck or belly rub and relax. She would then curl up in our laps, or back-to-back with Ollie on the couch.

We tried letting her have the run of the house but discovered early that her energy did not wane when the rest of us wanted to sleep at night. After a few overnights of being stalked in bed, any movement viewed as an invitation to pounce, and having toes attacked and chewed on, Heidi-Lou was assigned a bedtime in her foster room. (We continued to work on changing that behavior with behavioral training via a stuffed blue whale toy she loved.)

Each morning when Heidi-Lou would awaken, we would stir to the loud, pitiful cries begging for release from bondage and isolation from her room. Once free, she began the sad saga of a cat in need of nourishment. (Never mind her food left out the night before, or her dry bowl kept full.)

She'd been with us a month or so when her secondary vaccines came due. Off she went with Val to the vet's office with the promise to return in a couple of hours.

Although there was little to worry about, I still generally do when they leave until they are back and have the 'all clear.' Each time I offer a prayer that God will see them safely through.

Her second appointment away from us in foster was her scheduled spay a few weeks later. She did well and came home by the end of the day, but again I worried while she was gone. Spays for female cats are a much more invasive surgery than neuters for males. But just as with any surgery, until they are in recovery and starting to wake up from anesthesia, I am concerned and watch closely during their recovery stage. (Most veterinarians and reputable clinics won't release cats until they wake up and show no signs of complications.)

This also signaled that once she was healed (usually a week or two post spay), she would be eligible to return to the shelter for adoption. That was the most challenging part when fostering. It was hard to spend time working with them, teaching and loving them, and building that bond only to turn around and let them go. But that is always the intention, not to mention one of the biggest perks is that you've taught this cat what it's like to be loved. Thanks to their temporary time with you, they know what to expect from their forever home. (Love is patient and kind; love does not envy or boast; it is not arrogant or rude. It does not insist on its own way; it is not irritable or resentful; it does not rejoice at wrongdoing, but rejoices with the truth. 1 Corinthians 13:4–6)

In foster, like rescue, many times, they are one of many in a household sharing attention. By being adopted, she could move onto a home where she was chosen to become someone's special pet.

When Heidi-Lou returned, it was with the news that they believed she had either a large cyst or an infection deep inside her right ear. They had biopsied it and given an antibiotic injection if it was an infection, but she would require a follow-up exam after the 10 days for any infection to have healed. We hadn't noticed any telltale signs of hearing loss or an infection in her behavior, but that made it even better that they had found it in her exam.

Val asked if it was still good for her to return to us in foster, and we readily agreed. This was just a couple weeks past her expected departure, and so much better for her not to have to change environments again. It was concerning that the blockage in her ear might run the risk of rupture or become an issue with her long-term hearing, and we wanted to support her through it. There were certainly worse things kittens might have to deal with, but this could make it harder to place her through adoption if it did. I prayed God would allow her to heal and be healthy and normal. She had so much to give to a loving family, and I didn't want anything to prevent that for her.

Heidi-Lou was, without a doubt, a joy to have in the house and kept us laughing with her antics from day to day. She'd been with us long enough now to feel like a part of our family. In fact, she felt so at ease and blended into our pack that we began noticing some anarchy within the ranks. They were small things at first, a slight behavior outburst, competition over the feeding order, or a non-mutual game of chase down the hallway. The existing hierarchy our cats had established years ago was being disrupted as Heidi-Lou tried to find her place in the pack.

Unfortunately, rather than coming in and accepting last place, she had declared her intention to rise into the position above her, Kippy's.

Things escalated quickly between the two cats as Heidi-Lou pushed in a determined attempt to oust Kippy from her spot. Heidi-Lou chased her down the hall and jumped on her back in a display of dominance. At mealtimes, Heidi-Lou would push her way onto Kippy's plate in front of her. We heard hissing and yowling leading us to find Heidi-Lou backing Kippy into a corner. We might've expected worse results if Kippy had been a younger cat, still in her prime, but she was older now and had mellowed a bit with age.

Bringing in a new cat to an existing group always has risks involved. Our cats had been accustomed to others coming and going in some capacity. Still, we were always on the watch for any issues. In this case, although we loved Heidi-Lou and recognized she'd make a wonderful pet for adoption, Gregg and I agreed it wasn't suitable for the newest kitten to make Kippy feel uncomfortable in her own home. We'd let Val know it was time for her to move on.

The timing of Heidi-Lou's last check-up came at the right point for us all, and we arranged for her to go on to the next step in adoption. Her ear had cleared up well, and she was ready to find her forever home.

It was difficult to watch this sweet girl go, knowing she considered this her home now. We loved her, and the loss of her energy and light would be felt. I'm permanently moved to cry a little when these wonderful souls depart our care, missing their individual spirits and the precious bond we built. It's saying goodbye to a dear friend. For each foster baby that leaves our care, I remind myself of the fosters' motto: "I let my heart break a little so theirs will never be broken again."

With the departure of every foster or rescue soul, we send them off with a special prayer, knowing that they are safely returned to God's hands. We thank God for letting us be a part of their lives and a chapter in their stories. We are grateful for God's calling on our hearts that allows us to know and love precious souls. While the cat moves on, the fact that they are loved stays with us.

We appreciate God trusts us to have a role in their lives, to help groom them to be someone's beloved pet. As fosters, we strive to offer a foundation of love and the opportunity to include these souls in a home environment, making their transition, once adopted, easier.

Fostering can mean the difference between life and death for cats and provides the means to support rescues and shelters in their efforts to do more. Foster care for local shelters and rescues is always in demand.

There is always information on the internet about fostering and what it entails. It's essential to reach out to a reputable rescue in your area and speak directly about their foster program, as they can differ significantly. Each rescue and shelter has its own process and guidelines, with some more organized than others, so it's important to know what is required, and expected of a foster before you begin.

God wants us to respect and take care of animals. By fostering, you are saving lives and helping these souls with a second chance in life. Fostering is also a great exercise in so many ways:

- Provides love and care to an animal who may never have known this in their life.
- Frees up space at the shelter to allow the rescues to help more animals in need.
- Rescues animals from likely spending most of their time in a cage, or worse, on the streets.
- Gives cats in a shelter a break from institutional life and prevents them from developing bad habits.
- Allows cats with behavioral issues, traumatic experiences, or the need to be socialized in a better environment to recover
- Makes it easier to find a new home for a pet that has been living in a home environment with people and potentially other pets
- Provides a better environment for cats that are old, timid, sick, or recovering from an injury
- Is a wonderful way to get to know an animal well if you are considering adoption.

Whoever is righteous has regard for the life of his beast, but the mercy of the wicked is cruel.
Proverbs 12:10

The Secret Language of Rescue

God, grant me the serenity to accept the things I cannot change, courage to change the things I can, and wisdom to know the difference. —Reinhold Niebuhr

During WWII, thousands of women were recruited as covert 'code breakers' for the US Army and Navy working to provide critical intelligence information in the European and Pacific Theaters. They worked through a plethora of code and cipher systems to identify the real message behind the text that ultimately helped steer the war's outcome.

Rescuers often apply the same techniques in decoding and understanding the subtext and real meaning hidden behind the words when dealing with the public. Conversations can be wrapped up in pretty semantics and colorful rhetoric, chosen carefully to persuade and coerce the desired outcome, but the truth is the truth beneath it all. Through time and experience, most rescuers have learned the 'Language of Rescue,' and how to translate it into everyday language. Since repetition is the key to understanding any new language, I'm including the most common phrases and scenarios we've interpreted over the years.

The details may vary for each story, but an example of the most popular themes is included here:

(Taken from real encounters in rescue from Doodlebug Manor)

Cat Rental Conversation

- Caller: "*Hi. I'm wondering if ya'll have any cats that are good mousers*?"
- Rescue: "I'm not sure I understand the question, what is it you're looking for?"
- Caller: *"I have a barn, and I'm wondering what it would cost to rent a couple cats. We just need'em for a couple months."*
- Rescue: *"No, cats are not rental equipment, they*

are living souls. We do not rent cats."

Translation: *Do you have any cats (living souls) you've rescued, cared for, and loved that you would rent out to us like indentured servants to use for our purposes? We'd like you to remain responsible for them, but just let us use them.*

Boarding Cats

- Email: "We're going on vacation in Europe and need a place for our cats to go while we're gone. Can we board them with you? The boarding facilities are so expensive, they want pet records, and medications submitted; we're in a pinch as we're leaving tomorrow. Please call me immediately."
- Rescue: "We are a rescue group not equipped to board personal pets. I'm afraid we cannot board your cats. I can recommend some local boarding facilities. You can also hire a pet sitter to come to your home to care for them."

Translation: *We waited until the very last second to find someone to care for our pets, even though we've had months planning an overseas trip. We can afford Europe, but not to ensure our pets are cared for while we're gone. We don't want to provide their meds or vet records because it takes time. I need you to do this. Call me about it so I can try to pressure you into it.*

Take our Cat with Issues

- Caller: "Hi, I got your name from PetSmart and we need help. We have a 3-year-old cat who is peeing on the rugs and jumps up on the bed to go and it's making me crazy. We don't have time for this, so we need to surrender him. Can you take him and adopt him out? Yes, we declawed him."

- Rescue: "Has your cat been seen by the vet to rule out medical issues? This may be a temporary medical condition or behavioral issue. Did you declaw your cat? (In my head: *"What a coincidence, I have a list of people wanting to adopt cats with preexisting serious issues!?!?")*

Translation: *Our cat pees in the house and we don't want to take the time or spend the money to discover why or try to help him. You should fix this because you're a rescue. We want someone else to take responsibility even though we created the issue by declawing him.*

Moving

- Email: "Hello, we need your help. We are relocating out of town and need somewhere to place our elderly cats. We're moving in the morning to a different state and can't take our cats. We leave tomorrow and really need somewhere for them to go. Can you take them? They have nowhere else to go. Please let us know immediately."

- Rescue: "Good evening. Is there a reason you're unable to take your pets with you? If I may ask, why are you waiting until the night before to place them? I'm afraid we are not equipped to take in any cats now, as we are full. I would suggest placing them in boarding in the area you're going to until a permanent home can be found or reaching out to find a pet sitter in your new area." (In my head: *"Barring any new legislation I'm unaware of, cats are legal in all 50 states. For overseas, there is a naturalization process for pets.)"*

Translation: *We've spent the time planning to move, but never gave a thought to our elderly pets who rely on us, so now we just want to go and let someone else take care of this. We don't want to choose a place to live that allows pets in our new location.*

Matchy Matchy

- Email: "Hello. I'm looking to adopt a kitten. Do you have a Siamese, or any kitten in those smoky brown/cream tones? I need one that doesn't shed; I can't have cat dander in the house. I would need one that matches the couch and room décor and is declawed. Our last one was black and white, so I had to surrender her. Please let me know if you have one?"

- Rescue: "Hello, I'm afraid I can't assist you. Your requirements don't meet our process standards; we wouldn't adopt a cat out based on physical attributes. We also don't adopt to anyone who's surrendered their prior pet for those reasons, and our contract prohibits declawing. Most, if not all, cats shed, despite the rumors, so I would encourage you to think about if a living cat is really what you're looking for." (In my head: "*You can get the perfect cat that requires no care, no cleanup, no attention, and can sit atop your matching couch — it's in the toy section of Amazon for $69.99.")*

Translation: *I really want a cat that looks expensive, pretty, and matches my furniture. I am so much more concerned about the overall look of the cat as an accessory than personality or providing a safe, loving home for the cat. I specifically care more for my home furnishings than the health of a cat, so it will have to be declawed and if I change furniture again, I'll most likely surrender this cat as well.*

Replacement Cats

- Caller: "Hi, I'm looking for some cats to adopt. We recently lost our two barn cats to coyotes in the area and I wanted to see if you had any outdoor cats; we need some new ones."

- Rescue: "I'm so sorry for your loss, but no, this is one reason we don't adopt outdoor cats, we rarely have outdoor cats, and if we did, I could not adopt knowing you have a threat of coyotes that could kill them." (In my head: *!?!?!?!?!? I have no words. At least, luckily the county shelter won't adopt 'outdoor' cats to people.)*

Translation: *I just want some replacement cats for the ones the coyotes ate, and if these are eaten as well, that's just part of being outdoors. I won't do anything to protect them. There are a lot of cats in the world. We'll just keep replacing them.*

Pay My Utilities Since You're Nonprofit

- Email: Hi, I'm hoping you can help me. My son needs help to pay his utility bills this month. He had some expenses with his dog and now he's behind on his bills. You're nonprofit; could you help him out?

- Rescue: *No, our charter does not cover extending donations to support people's living expenses. Our purpose is to help cats in need.*

Translation: *My son did the right thing helping his dog and now deserves someone to cover his bills for him. You're a nonprofit, so you should help him and pay for it.*

I'll Ruin Your Rescue

- Email: I filled out an adoption application with your group and the person who worked with me was rude. She told me no, like I'm not good enough for one of your cats? I want the manager to return a call to me. I'll report you and make sure I ruin your rescue.

- Rescue: I'm sorry if you felt like our group was rude to you. I have the email trail of your denial and I'm afraid it is based on our conditions for adoption. You indicated you plan to declaw, and to allow the cat outside. Also, I am the Director ma'am.

Translation: *I didn't get what I wanted, and I will be difficult until you change your mind and do as I want. This has been my way of treating people whenever I don't get my way for a very long time, and I see no need to move any differently now!*

There are so many things that rescuers encounter within the realm of animal care. Some are odd, or surprising, sometimes with hindsight they are funny. Many times, they are disheartening, defeating, and infuriating. Things go awry regardless of your level of dedication or best efforts. It can be difficult to understand and not to get stuck in the notion that all bad things that befall our animal friends begin and end at our door, humans.

God loves all His children, the animals are our brethren. We are all His children protected by the covenant he made with Noah. (Behold, I establish my covenant with you and your offspring after you, and with every living creature that is with you, the birds, the livestock, and every beast of the earth with you, as many as came out of the ark; it is for every beast of the earth. I establish my covenant with you, that never again shall all flesh be cut off by the waters of the flood, and never again shall there be a flood to destroy the earth. Genesis 9:9–11)

At times, it is exceedingly challenging to forgive the acts of cruelty, neglect, and evil within the arena where you are most passionate. The same calling on your heart to work for God's animals calls out so strongly when you feel the injustice of wrongdoing. That is when God reminds us, in Romans 12:19, that we are not to take revenge, but to leave room for the wrath of God. We are never to pay back evil for evil to anyone. Respect what is right in the sight of all men.

God made us all. He knows our hearts, and He feels the pain and anguish we feel. As Christians, we are expected to follow the example Christ sets, to love and forgive one another just as Christ does for us. (Be kind to one another, tenderhearted, forgiving one another, as God in Christ forgave you. Ephesians 4:32) In doing so, God will heal our hearts and refill our spirit. We can overcome and the Peace of the Lord fills us, and begin again another day, setting His example of love in the world. (In the same way, let your light shine before others, so that they may see your good works and give glory to your Father who is in heaven. Matthew 5:16)

God's got this, and our role as Christians is to continue to persevere as overcomers for His Kingdom.

> For God so loved the world, that he gave his only Son, that whoever believes in him should not perish but have eternal life. For God did not send his Son into the world to condemn the world, but in order that the world might be saved through him. John 3:16–17

> Put on then, as God's chosen ones, holy and beloved, compassionate hearts, kindness, humility, meekness, and patience; Colossians 3:12

> Beloved, never avenge yourselves, but leave it to the wrath of God, for it is written, "Vengeance is mine, I will repay, says the Lord." Romans 12:19

Endnotes

1. One of the premier groups we found online to learn about trapping, and all things 'feral' was a group called Alley Cat Allies. (https://www.alleycat.org) They are an international group dedicated to advocacy for cats and improving their lives and are still very active today. An additional resource to learn about cats & kittens is through Kitten Lady, Hannah Shaw, via her YouTube Video Channel Kitten Lady. https://www.youtube.com/kittenlady

2. The virus spreads from one cat to another via saliva and bodily fluids through various contact forms. This makes the infection more prevalent in high-risk populations, such as cats with outdoor access and/or frequent social interactions. The age and time of infection affect the progression of the virus. Mothers' milk is one of the main fluids through which it transmits, making kittens extremely susceptible to infection and developing more severe complications.

3. A great reference to learn more about the necessary FVRCP vaccinations is via PetMD online at: What Is the FVRCP Cat Vaccine? https://www.petmd.com/cat/wellness/what-fvrcp-cat-vaccine

4. FIV attacks the immune system, leaving the cat vulnerable to many other infections. Although cats infected with FIV may appear normal for years, eventually, they may suffer from immune deficiency, which allows normally harmless bacteria, viruses, protozoa, and fungi found in the everyday environment to cause severe illnesses. There is no cure for FIV. Recent studies suggest indoor cats with FIV commonly live average life spans.
   The primary transmission mode for FIV is through bite wounds from an infected cat. Casual, nonaggressive contact, such as sharing water bowls or mutual grooming, does not appear to be an efficient route of spreading the virus. As a result, cats in households with stable social structures where housemates do not fight are at little risk of acquiring FIV infections. ~ Cornell Feline Health Center

5. Pet Sitters International is an educational association for professional pet sitters that represents nearly 7,000 independent professionals, and a source for pet owners to find licensed, bonded sitters. Pet Sitters International, the leading pet-sitter association. https://www.petsit.com

6. Animal Rescue Corps -They specialize in re-

sponding to cases of severe neglect, abandonment, and cruelty where they work to remove the animals from the horrendous conditions they are in and bring them back to their rehab facility, where volunteers and veterinarians care for these animals. Volunteers work to provide for the physical, emotional, and behavioral needs of the animals until they are healed enough to be eligible for rehoming. Coordinators then work with Humane Associations and rescues throughout the U.S. to place these animals for adoption. (They are a wonderful, worthy cause and a 501 (c) (3) relying on public support and donations to do the work they do.) https://animalrescuecorps.org/

7. Cerebellar Hypoplasia Cats and Kittens | Facebook

Additional Resources

Emory Winship Cancer Institute: To learn more about FeLV visit Emory University online at https://www.cancerquest.org/

Adoptapet.com: Rehoming program built into its adoption site incentivizes rescues to help owners place surrendered cats through their program.

The Blue Bell Foundation for Cats: offers loving and compassionate lifetime care for senior cats whose owners can no longer care for them. bluebellcats.org

Hearts that Purr Feline Guardians: offers a lifetime care program for Senior Cats, and Estate Planning. heartsthatpurr.org

The CATS Cradle Shelter: a long-term care foster program for senior cats to live out their care in the comfort of a typical domestic setting. catscradleshelter.org

Stay in touch with Lara and the work that she is doing through her books, speaking engagements and guest podcast appearances at Facebook Lara Germony | Facebook, and cat rescue on via Facebook Doodlebug Manor Cat Rescue 501c3 and Instagram @LaraGermony. Join her on the journey of the latest rescue at her rescue shelter's website at Doo odlebugmanor@webs.com.

Made in the USA
Columbia, SC
30 January 2024